A Little Bird Told Me...

KASEY CHAMBERS

With Jeff Apter

HarperCollins*Publishers*

HarperCollins*Publishers*

First published in Australia in 2011
by HarperCollins*Publishers* Australia Pty Limited
ABN 36 009 913 517
harpercollins.com.au

HarperCollins*Publishers*
Level 13, 201 Elizabeth Street, Sydney NSW 2000, Australia
31 View Road, Glenfield, Auckland 0627, New Zealand
A 53, Sector 57, Noida, UP, India
77–85 Fulham Palace Road, London, W6 8JB, United Kingdom
2 Bloor Street East, 20th floor, Toronto, Ontario M4W 1A8, Canada
10 East 53rd Street, New York NY 10022, USA

National Library of Australia Cataloguing-in-Publication entry

Chambers, Kasey.
A little bird told me / Kasey Chambers with Jeff Apter.
ISBN: 978 0 7322 9108 2 (pbk.)
Chambers, Kasey.
Country musicians – Australia – Biography
Other Authors/Contributors: Apter, Jeff, 1961–
781.642092

Cover design by Jane Waterhouse, HarperCollins Design Studio
Cover photograph by Amanda Toombs reproduced by permission of Chambers Entertainment
Back cover photograph from a family collection reproduced by permission of Kasey Chambers
Typeset in 11.5/18pt Adobe Caslon by Kirby Jones
Printed and bound in Australia by Griffin Press
60gsm Hi Bulk Book Cream used by HarperCollins*Publishers* is a natural, recyclable product
made from wood grown in sustainable forests. The manufacturing processes conform to the
environmental regulations in the country of origin, Finland.

5 4 3 2 1   11 12 13 14

This book is dedicated to:

My mum: I thank you for the strength, the friendship,
the forgiveness, the positivity and the wonderful gift
of how to be the best mother I can be.

My dad: I thank you for the laughter, the music,
the understanding and the Chambers way of life.

And Nash: I thank you for the opportunities, the drive,
the hard work, the level head — and most of all for
always putting your sister before the career.

A big thank you to:

Jeff for helping my story come to life; and a special thank
you to Shane, Talon and Arlo for making every day just
what it should be. And thanks to everyone who's been
part of my journey (so far).

Contents

Prologue

It might seem a bit cheeky for me to write my life story at the age of 34. There are moments when I think I should wait a few more years, after all what's the hurry? But I've thought a lot about the reasons behind why I'm doing this and it feels like it is the right time. On one level the book is an extension of what I do for a living; share my life with people, sometimes through my songs – in which I've always tried to be as honest as possible – but mostly just through talking to others. Some people play golf, others love camping; my favourite pastime is talking. I love meeting people, being around people, connecting with people. And I feel that my story is worth sharing; in fact, I believe that everyone's story is worth sharing, if you feel comfortable enough to do it.

I've never been one to sugarcoat things too much; I think the only way to genuinely relate to people is to be true to yourself, and about yourself. This means revealing the good and the bad. Even though I know that a lot of my life story and experiences are different because of circumstances, and because what I do is so public, I also know that many people can strongly relate to what I've been through. I hope that someone reading might feel 'Wow, I'm not alone', or, perhaps, 'I know what that feels like.' Maybe some of the things in here will also make them laugh; along with some tough times, I've had a lot of fun.

Writing this book brought home how the things I take for granted as 'normal life' will feel like anything but that to a lot of people. But I've also had constants, and the biggest of those is my family. It's not just that we are close, we are a team, in music and in life.

There is my immediate family: Dad and Mum – Bill and Diane Chambers – and my elder brother, Nash. There's my adult family: my husband, Shane, and my two boys, Talon and Arlo, plus our new baby, due in October 2011. And, sorry to confuse you, but there's also Talon's father, Cori, and my best friend, Worm, who is definitely one of us. And in my home town of Southend, South Australia, there was the giant Chambers clan, but I'll get to that later.

I never take for granted the rare opportunities I have had, and the wonderful, beautiful people who I've shared my life with. All of them have contributed to make me the person that I am today – the person I am happy to be. There have been many, many occasions where I've had to pinch myself, just to make sure that it really is me, doing what I love, and doing it on my own terms. Even if I could, I wouldn't change a thing. And I look forward to somehow being able to share the next chapter of my life with you, too.

Avoca Beach Hotel
Thursday, 12 July 2007

'Hello, everyone, and welcome to another Lost Dogs night. By the way, I have an announcement to make: I'm in labour. Two centimetres dilated. If my water breaks during the gig, and I have to be rushed to hospital, I apologise now. For your sakes, I hope that won't happen.'

I've played thousands of shows in my life – I've been performing on stage since I was nine years old – but this gig, at my local pub, has to rank with one of the weirdest. Good common sense suggests that it's not the best idea to get up and sing with a band when you're nine months pregnant, ten days overdue and bigger than a barn, but there was something about my gigs with the Lost Dogs band that I found impossible to resist. They were a reminder of why I'd fallen in love with music in the first place. And, frankly, I was just about over the whole pregnancy thing; maybe if I sang Patty Griffin's 'Top of the World' at the top of my lungs – an old favourite and a Lost Dogs standard – it might speed up my baby's entry into the world, although hopefully in not too graphic a way. After all, this was a dining room; people were eating here!

So there I was on this freezing cold night, dressed in my leggings and fitted top – the only things I could squeeze into by then – singing my favourite songs with many of my favourite musicians. The crowd were the usual shaggy Lost Dogs crowd; other musos, locals who called out the tunes they wanted to hear and, of course, many of the Chambers family. It was an upbeat, comfortable, slightly chaotic atmosphere, the sort of gig I'd grown up playing.

What most of those around me didn't know was that I was coming to the end of one of the most difficult and turbulent periods of my life. I'd released my fourth album, called *Carnival*, in 2006, and as usual I'd managed to smile and laugh my way through the round of interviews and gigs. But underneath it all I had slowly been coming undone.

Any musician who is being honest will admit that there comes a time when the line blurs between doing what you love and letting it become just a job. It's an age-old struggle and one that I thought I'd managed to stay on the right side of. But somewhere, without me seeing it, the lines had blurred for me and music had become just another job. One I could do well – I hope – but something which no longer brought me any joy.

I had reached a point where I didn't want to be a musician any more, where the things I'd loved all my life – singing, writing, playing – had become the things I least wanted to do. I had to psych myself up to play gigs, to fight off the feeling that people didn't really care what I sang, that they were just coming to see a name, someone called 'Kasey Chambers'. At home, I didn't want to listen to music at all; I'd flip out when my husband, Shane, dared to play a record at the home we share on the NSW Central Coast.

It had taken a big toll on me. Up till then I'd been generally a pretty happy person and a healthy eater. But when these feelings started getting the better of me, I became a new me, a me I didn't much like. I was miserable, paranoid, I felt so odd. And over a year, I gradually stopped eating. My weight plummeted to 44 kilos, about ten kilos below my ideal weight. I was alternately starving myself and over-eating, forcibly throwing up most of the food that I did eat. Strangest of all, I had become a hardcore exercise junkie, running each day for kilometres, burning off what little weight I actually possessed. And as anyone who knows me would tell you, I really hate exercise. Hate it. I was never sporty at school or anything like that. Yet time after time I'd leave our house, wearing sunglasses in case anyone recognised me – hah! – and jog about a kilometre to a spot near my house called Captain Cook Lookout. There was public access there, with this really incredible view, but I hadn't come for the vista. I'd sneak under the fence and scale down the cliff to this quite dangerous ledge, and just sit there. Then I'd cry and cry and cry.

Hindsight is a wonderful thing, and in time I've come to understand some of the underlying things that brought me to this terrible, dangerous stage. It had nothing to do with body image; my career has never been based on my looks. Yes, my biggest song to date was titled 'Not Pretty Enough', but although I've sometimes felt like an outsider in the music industry, as the song suggests, the truth is I'm okay with the way I look.

No, much of my disorder came out of a simple feeling – control, or rather the lack of it. Throughout my career I've never really been able to say no – especially if I was asked nicely. I've never taken a lengthy break from the cycle of recording and touring. And because I feel blessed in what I do, I figured I had no reason to complain – plus I hate hearing other artists whining about their hard life. I mean, what is so hard about writing and singing songs? So I let the pressure build and build and build and eventually it ate me up. I woke up one day and felt as though all this accumulated stress had swallowed me whole. There was a huge burden on my head, and it manifested itself in my eating disorder. I may not have been able to control what happened with my music career, I figured, but I can damn well control what I put in my mouth. It was crazy thinking. And I was the only person I could blame for my meltdown.

I was in complete denial about my disease until one day my brother, Nash, who also manages my career, produces my records and does his best to shield me from the business side of music, came to my house with a pretty straightforward promotional request from my record label. I suddenly burst into tears. My mother, Diane, who was there too, had been watching me brush off questions about my health for a while from Shane and others, and I think she knew that I might be ready to face facts.

'Are you really okay?' they both asked.

I knew what I had to say, but it was just so difficult speaking the words, even to the two people in the world who knew me better than anyone else. It seemed like years passed before I gathered the courage to reply.

'I'm not,' I finally said. 'I think I have an eating disorder. I think I need to get some help.'

Mum and Nash weren't really shocked. Everyone close to me could see the state I was in, both physically and emotionally, but they had the great sense to wait for me to admit to my problem. My mum, who always knows what to say at exactly the right time, held me in her arms and let me sob. 'Yes,' she said, simply. 'I think you do.'

It took many months of therapy and recovery for me to even think about the role that music should again play in my life. As I slowly improved – and purely on a whim – I decided, along with Shane and my dad, Bill Chambers, to form a band. But this was a band with a difference: we were going to play the songs that we've always loved, the kind of music we'd like to hear from a band playing down the pub. We became the Lost Dogs, and lost dogs we were, in some respects. Especially me.

Everything about the Lost Dogs was in defiance of what I'd become used to over the past few years. We'd only play other people's songs. We didn't rehearse. No two sets were the same. There was no set list. There was no hogging the microphone. The core of the band was us three, with the help of Chris Haigh on bass, but there'd be different players and special guests every week.

I was one-third of a band now, not Kasey Chambers the solo act, and I loved that. I was a back-up singer for two-thirds of the night, and I loved that too. It was so good, so badly what I'd needed after possibly the darkest time of my life. We constantly messed songs up, but that didn't matter. For the first time in as long as I could remember, it felt as though there were no expectations on me at all. All I had to do was turn up and play, and share jokes with the band and the crowd, as we stumbled through our favourite songs. On a good night, Shane and I cleared enough money from the gig to pay for that week's groceries. Given that I wasn't really working at the time, this cash came in handy!

What started as a musical experiment ran for almost a year, most of which time I was pregnant with my second child. I got to know the regulars in the audience so well that I'd tell them about my visits to the doctors, my ultrasounds, the works. It was such a great, healing time in my life, as two big things happened: my child grew inside me and my love for music slowly returned.

The week before my due date, I updated the 100 or so people who were at the gig that Thursday night. 'Hopefully I won't be here next week,' I said, 'but I'll put pregnancy updates on my website. Shane and Dad will still be here, unless I'm actually in labour – then Shane is with me.'

However, that week passed and there I was, back on the stool, seated alongside my fellow Lost Dogs, still very pregnant. On the day of the Avoca gig, I'd been to the hospital for a progress report, and they broke the news that I was actually two centimetres dilated. 'You're in labour, you know,' the nurse told me with a smile. 'It'll still be some time, though, so go home and put your feet up.'

But Thursday night was 'Lost Dogs night', as we'd all come to call it, and I couldn't sit around at home while the band played without me. No way. Everyone seemed a little surprised when I turned up, although I'm sure that I put the band and the crowd at ease when I apologised in advance, in case my water broke during the gig.

It took a few more days before Arlo Ray – named after the singer Arlo Guthrie and Shane's dad, Ray – finally appeared, but he was with me two Thursdays later when I returned for that week's Lost Dogs show. I was hobbling around because of my emergency C-section, but I didn't mind. I was with my baby boy and surrounded by my husband, family and friends. No more lost dog; I had found my way home.

1

Nullarbor

When I was a little girl
I had the biggest backyard in the world
Covered up with red dirt as far as I could see
I shared it with the railway and the Aborigines
Southwest of Ooldea
All the way down to the sea and back.

Lyrics from 'Nullarbor, the Biggest Backyard'

I don't remember seeing the Nullarbor for the first time; my introduction took place when I was just three weeks old. A lot of my memories have become tied up with the stories and recollections my parents have, so the pictures I draw in my head may not be entirely mine. But I know that early on I developed an addiction to its vastness and silence and sudden, stark beauty. It's a place whose smells and sounds I recall vividly, the place that formed me. For the first ten years of my life, from 1976 to 1986, it's the place I thought of as home.

Whenever I was awake, I was laughing, smiling, singing, constantly on the lookout for new Nullarbor experiences and adventures. I loved my parents and I had absolutely no doubt that they loved me. I loved my brother, Nash, and he loved me right back, even if he expressed it in a pinching, punching, name-calling, big-brotherly kind of way. But I knew better. We were best friends. We had to be. For eight months of every year we awoke in a different place in the desert almost every morning, nearly always alone, usually hundreds of kilometres from civilisation, and yet it never felt foreign. Anywhere on the massive, sprawling, daunting Nullarbor Plain felt like home to me.

When we would go back to our home in Southend, SA, which we would do for a few months each year, I'd be perfectly happy among my friends and family there, but it felt like filling in time until we got to go outback again. Because really, as a young kid, you couldn't have asked for a more exciting existence.

It's not too hard to describe the visual characteristics of the Nullarbor – flat red dirt, salt and blue bush, mercilessly dry – but it is hard to find the right words to accurately capture one of the most amazing, isolated and captivating spots on earth, a place I was lucky enough to call my backyard. I can tell you this – it was one bloody big backyard. Let me try, anyway: the Nullarbor was remote but never lonely, unaffected but not backward, sparse yet not empty, unpredictable, sometimes dangerous, but so, so comforting.

Now that I am a mother myself, I can better appreciate how my mum must have felt about going outback to the Nullarbor, sleeping under the stars with small children in tow. Sure, it was a grand adventure. It was also hot, dry, dusty. At that time there were no roads to speak of. No shops. No hospitals if someone got sick, no bathroom to wash in. It was at least two days drive back to Southend, often more. She would have had to defend the scheme to her family who thought it was insane – and to Dad's family – who agreed. But Mum and Dad shared a certain wilful, restless spirit, which helped, because there were times when it was more of a Wild West ride.

One time, when Mum was eight months pregnant with me, Dad was spotted on someone's station property. Okay, he was poaching. The landowner came out with a shotgun and jumped in his ute to give chase. Dad, with Mum and a terrified three-year-old Nash in the car, drove off at full pelt, about 140 ks an hour, with this guy in hot pursuit, firing at our Jeep. Gravel was flying everywhere. Just when Dad thought he was in the clear, our car started running out of petrol.

Dad kept a jerry can of fuel and a hose in the back of the Jeep.

'Di,' he yelled, 'you're gonna have to open the back door and siphon some fuel into the tank.' Mum had never done this before.

'It's easy,' shouted Dad. 'Just put the hose in the jerry can and suck until the petrol comes out.' Easy!

Fortunately, the fuel inlet was near the back door of the Jeep; she could reach it by opening the door and leaning out. So there was my very pregnant mum, leaning out to siphon the fuel from the jerry can into the tank, and all the while Dad kept driving and dodging the angry farmer's bullets. Just as our car started to stall, the engine kicked over and they got away. I wasn't yet born and I'd had my first close call.

Nullarbor is derived from the Latin term *nullus arbor*, meaning 'no trees', and that's exactly what I saw most mornings when I awoke. I'd look out over miles upon miles of flat, treeless plains, red dirt and blue bush as far as my young eyes could see. This landscape stretched seemingly forever – it was as if the horizon eventually blended into the sky itself. On a calm day I sometimes felt like I was looking out over a red dirt ocean. But, frankly, when I was a little kid, scenery didn't mean that much to me: how was I to know that this remarkable image would become one of my most vivid childhood memories? For me, it was just another day in my red desert paradise.

We travelled in the Landcruiser and we slept in the Landcruiser, where Nash and I had little bunks next to Mum and Dad's double bed. Behind us, we towed a mini-caravan or trailer which was part dining room and storage space for food and water and part Dad's working space. Originally there had been a larger caravan in tow but one trip with multiple punctures along the bush tracks put an end to that – from then on we travelled light.

My dad was a fox hunter.

By the time I was born, fox hunting was already a big part of my parents' lives; they would trek out to the big cattle stations on the outskirts of the Nullarbor with Nash, shoot the foxes whose pelts they could sell to Adelaide- or Melbourne-based buyers for around $20 each and then come back to Southend for a few short months with a nice bit of cash in their pockets.

For Dad, the working days went late. Once he'd worked out where the foxes were – and they could be anywhere in the area from Roxbury Downs to Kalgoorlie in Western Australia – he would hunt all night. That meant driving the old car with all of us inside, in hot pursuit over saltbush and sand with the suspension crashing up and down, the constant firing of guns, spotlights flashing on and off. Amazingly, Nash and I, who went to bed an hour or two into the night, slept through the tremendous nightly racket, tucked up in our bunks. Nothing disturbed us. To this day I can sleep through anything, anywhere and I generally like the TV on when I sleep.

On the nights we were hunting, which was any night there were foxes and the weather was fine, Mum rode up front with Dad and helped him with the spotlight which he'd shine on foxes. Eventually she'd turn in too and he'd continue until he'd got the number of foxes he wanted – his personal best was 44. Then, usually around 2 am, he'd drive back to where we'd set up camp with the trailer and he'd finally get to bed. When Nash and I woke up – usually pretty early – we were allowed to get up and around on our own but the one rule was that we Could Not Disturb Dad.

So each morning I had to be very careful and extremely quiet as I crawled over the bunk of my parents and shuffled past Nash. I was especially wary of Dad who really needed his sleep. In fact, one of the few times I can recall seeing my dad mad – and to this day he is one mellow fellow – was when Nash or I interrupted his morning snooze.

My parents were very tolerant and understanding with us, but Mum always gave Nash and me this one warning: 'Whatever you do in the morning – and it's fine if you get up and take a look about – don't wake up Dad. Okay?' Fortunately, Dad slept on the far side of the bunk, so if I accidentally disturbed anyone, it was Mum.

Typically, I'd give Nash a gentle nudge on my way through the car, in the hope that he would wake up and keep me company. After all, this was the best part of the day – peering out of the driver's side window and discovering where we were and then exploring today's new camp for the first time. As part of his work, Dad would drive through the night, sometimes covering hundreds of kilometres, so we'd awake in a totally new part of the sprawling Nullarbor. We would move camp almost every evening to a new spot.

When I was older, us kids started to develop our own routines. In the morning we'd have a few chores like collecting firewood – I say chores, but really, it was a game – and then some correspondence school lessons that Mum taught us. Then we were free to do what we wanted, which most days meant building a cubby house from Dad's unused fox boards, or if we were lucky, from a half tree we might find. Trees were unusual out there but occasionally we'd come across a clump of them and that's where we'd make our nightly camp.

To build a cubby, we'd start with one of the plywood planks on which Dad would pin the fox skins before drying them, which are about 50 centimetres wide and 100 centimetres high, and place it between two bushes. Sometimes it worked out great, but sometimes the surrounds could be pretty lame and we knew we were in for a bad 'cubby day'. But if there was plenty of surrounding bush, then we'd be fine.

Sometimes we'd find half a tree, which could easily be made into a cubby – now that was exciting! Apart from our school lessons, most of our days were spent in and around these cubbies, playing typical kids' games. I had no real concept of time whatsoever while out on the desert. (I'm the exact opposite now: I'm early for everything and if someone is late it drives me crazy.) The closest thing we had to a real idea of time was the moment when Mum would yell out that lunch was ready, or that it was time for our bath.

Nash, who is three years older than me and very much a boy, would probably have preferred to go off on his own with his bow and arrow or his slug gun, but he was pretty good about letting me tag along behind him for games of chasies or Cowboys and Indians. He didn't have much choice, frankly. We did have some other playmates – our cousins Narelle, Traci and Clint – the children of Dad's cousin, Gary, and his wife, Val Chambers, who were fellow hunters with us on these trips. But for the most part, Nash and I were constant companions, and best mates by default.

Mum tells me that I was an easy kid with a sunny temper. A bit of a tomboy – which I had to be because of the environment – with many of the character traits I still have today. I wasn't much good at school – I waited impatiently for the hour or so of lessons to be over so I could get out and play. I wanted to be part of everything, whether it was trailing in Nash's wake or helping Dad put the primer into his homemade bullets.

As Seventh Day Adventists, which we were at that point, we regarded Saturday as the Sabbath so between Friday sundown and Saturday sundown we didn't work. Our cousins were not religious so on those nights they would move on to the next hunting spot, but we stayed in the same place overnight. Normally we'd be packing up and rushing off so this was a welcome time to relax. On Fridays it was so nice to just sit there, around the fire, taking everything in. Then, all of a sudden, it would turn dark and the sky would turn on its light show. It was kind of magical, really.

Best of all, after dinner we would sit around the campfire singing while Dad played his guitar. It sounds like a country song – and in fact it *was* a country song: Johnny Cash's 'Daddy Sang Bass', about a family who sang together – one of our favourites. I loved it because I had a line of my own: 'Me and little brother would join right in'. The rest of the song was just marking time until I got to sing my bit – my attraction to the stage kicking in early. Already I was a bit of a ham.

People often ask if I had a musical education or music lessons, and the answer is, not really. Music wasn't something we learned; it was a totally natural part of our lives – as it still is. These days my kids sing with the band, or sing along with Shane and me at home if we're jamming, but I've never put pressure on them to have lessons. There was none of that pressure for me either as a child.

I sang because it was the thing we all did; back then, if someone told me that they didn't sit around the campfire as a family and sing and play the guitar, I would ask: 'So what do you do for fun?'

I guess I was getting an education of sorts from Dad, who is always happy to talk about music. Some nights when we were out hunting, and Nash and Mum were asleep, I'd wake up and sneak up front to sit alongside Dad while he worked. I recall those nights with great fondness; an incredibly strong bond formed between Dad and me, a special connection that remains to this day.

I'd help him with the spotlight for the foxes so I got to feel part of what he was doing. 'Spotlighting' worked like this: when we'd see a fox, we'd have to 'whistle' it up to the car – Dad carried a whistle, and I did, too, while Dad had also recorded a fox whistle on both sides of a C90 cassette, which he played on speakers mounted to the outside of the car as we drove through the night. (He's a very practical man, my dad.) We'd whistle the fox up to the car, and as Dad did that, I was allowed to take over the spotlight, which was fixed to the roof of the Landcruiser. The trick was that you had to put the spotlight in front of the animal. If you shone the light straight on its body, or in its eyes, it would panic and run back into the dark. But by shining the light just in front you were drawing the animal closer to you. Then, when Dad had the fox in his sights, he'd say, 'Now!' and I'd point the spotlight directly at the fox. It was crucial to be totally still when you did that.

Our poodle, Licky, was also a big help at night. Like the rest of us, he was totally up for adventure. He was a shaggy dog, always covered in burrs and dust, not some pampered poodle. And Licky was a surprisingly good hunting dog. He was curious, too; sometimes he'd head down holes, which were pretty common, and get chased out by wombats, who'd be very pissed off by Licky's home invasion. When we'd shoot something, Dad would open the door and Licky would retrieve it. Sometimes Dad would forget where the shot foxes were and Licky would go and find them. But every now and again Licky would come across a fox that wasn't quite dead yet and he'd get attacked. I once had to push him around in a doll's pram, which was about the only girly thing I had out there, because his leg was bunged up from an attack.

This reminds me of a funny story. When the 20-year-old son of a fox buyer briefly joined us out on the Nullarbor, he brought along his puppy, which I adored. Innocently, I asked him what he called the dog, and he matter-of-factly replied: 'Oh, I just call it a little cunt.' So I figured that the dog's name was Cunt – I was a kid, I'd never heard the word before, I didn't know any better, so I accepted it as the truth. There I was, running around the desert, calling out for 'Cunt', with total naïveté, while my dog, Licky, trailed behind. Looking back, it's like the punch line for some really obscene joke: two dogs called Cunt and Licky. I'm not sure if Mum or Dad ever heard me calling out, or maybe they were in on the gag; I can't say it's something we've ever discussed! (For a while we also had a pet kangaroo, but I can't recall that he had a dodgy nickname.)

Anyway, during those nights with Dad I got to listen to the kind of high lonesome country music he loved playing on the car's tape deck. He would tell me the stories behind it: where Johnny Cash came from, who Merle Haggard was and how he had gone to San Quentin prison for robbery. These people became mythical figures to me; it was hard to believe that they really existed.

One night, Dad told me a story about appearing on the TV show *New Faces*. His reputation as a muso didn't extend much beyond his local area, so to appear on a national TV show was a huge achievement.

'There was this comedian on the same show,' Dad said. 'His name was Paul Hogan.'

'Oh yeah?' I asked with complete ignorance. 'What does he do now?'

'He's a big movie star,' said Dad.

I turned to Dad and said, in all seriousness: 'You really showed him, Dad.'

Dad thinks of music as his cultural heritage – whether it's American, English or Australian – and he wanted to pass that heritage on to Nash and me. Many of Dad's records remain among my favourites – Dan Fogelberg's *High Country Snows*; Ricky Skaggs's *Highways & Heartaches*; *Waylon & Willie*; Gram Parsons's *GP* – I especially loved the song 'Still Feeling Blue', which I'd one day cover – the Amazing Rhythm Aces's self-titled LP, the Gatlin Brothers – rootsy things like that. And if I was really lucky on those nights in the Landcruiser, Dad would even let me play the first tape that I ever bought with my own money:

Father Abraham in Smurfland. 'Smurfing Beer' was my favourite song, with its brilliant lyrics:

> *Beer, beer, smurfing beer*
> *You don't get drunk*
> *And it isn't dear.*

There were plenty of potential dangers out in the Nullarbor, though we kids didn't think much about them. Mum and Dad did their fair share of worrying over what could happen to Nash or me, given the huge trapdoor spiders and western taipans, snakes that would come straight at you if they were disturbed. One morning we found a taipan in the firewood on the roof after a really hot night, when we'd slept with the removable sunroof open hoping to catch a breeze. There were also the dingoes, which would sometimes walk right up to our camp and snatch the dead foxes hanging from the bull bar. They were cagey, cheeky animals, not to be messed with.

We also had to be wary of the many caves that dotted the landscape. Okay, technically speaking they weren't caves, they were bloody big holes in the ground, but we called them caves. They were really, really deep; big enough to swallow a car. If you accidentally drove into one, that would be the end of you. No one would know where you were. Whenever Dad saw a cave he'd mark it down on the map, so that next year when we returned we knew to be extra careful. We'd always check out these holes. We all shared this eerie sense: 'What would happen if we drove into one?' That was as close as I came to feeling scared out there. Nash always had a packet of matches so that if we ever did get lost we could light a piece of bush and alert people to our whereabouts with smoke signals, but that wouldn't have helped much at the bottom of a hole.

If we came across a cave during the daytime, we were allowed to explore it – with Mum and Dad, of course. One time we went down into a cave, and found that there were a series of other caves leading off the main one. Not long after, the Army were out there doing some sort of manoeuvres, and they went into the same cave and found an opalised snapper, hanging from the roof of the cave, in its full and ancient form. I heard a rumour that they sold it on the black market – so they could keep the money themselves – for a million dollars.

Inevitably, there were accidents. I once fell out of one of the Nullarbor's few trees, and fractured my ankle, although we didn't find out the extent of my injury until much, much later. To help me get around, Dad fashioned some crutches out of dead tree branches and added some cloth for support, and I stumbled around for the next few weeks until my ankle sort of healed, although it still gives me grief when the weather turns cold. That was typical of how we lived out there – improvisational skills were essential if we were to survive. Another time I came down with whooping cough, so we simply drove the 200 or so miles across country, through the scrub, steering by compass and the stars, Dad's usual method, until we met the Flying Doctor Service at the Cook railway crossing. Now that was a long night.

We were raised around weapons – Dad had several rifles that he used in his work and we were constantly warned about their dangers. Dad was very careful; although his rifles were stored in the car, in racks, they were never loaded. Firearms were around all the time, they were a part of our lives, so they didn't really faze us – and we also knew to respect them. He had a .22 Hornet Anschutz, which he used for close- to medium-range shooting; a custom-made Walther .17, that was best for long-range targets; and a .222 Tika that was ideal for up to about 250 metres. (When we hunted rabbits he used a .22 Rimfire rifle.) We weren't allowed to touch his rifles, although Nash and I would shoot targets with a slug gun, and sometimes even 'top notch' pigeons, with Dad watching over us. Then we'd eat the pigeons, which were really tasty.

I had a small pocketknife, which I carried with me, but Dad wouldn't let me skin the foxes; that was serious work and not for kids. But he would allow me to put the primer into his bullets. (Dad truly was a practical, DIY kind of guy – I mean, how many kids have fathers who made their own bullets?) I'm sure, thinking back, that he only let me help because I complained long and loud enough, but I do remember it as a real thrill. Dad would put the gunpowder into the casing, Nash would do his bit and then I'd help out. It was an odd thing for a little girl to do, I guess, but I really wanted to be involved with whatever was going on.

Nash's bow and arrow set wasn't a toy; it was a real weapon with sharpened tips, perfect for shooting targets. I wasn't allowed to use his, although I had my own bow and arrow set, but the tips weren't sharpened. During our annual Christmas holiday, when the entire Chambers clan would get together, usually at Lake George, not far from Beachport, we'd be allowed to shoot wild ducks – and let me just say that you can't beat camp-oven duck, cooked over the coals of an open fire. Another annual family get-together was at Border Village, at Eucla, on the coast near the borders of South and Western Australia. We had nowhere to store the fish we caught there, so we'd light a fire down a rabbit hole, lay the fillets across the opening and smoke them. I guess not many people can claim to have eaten fish that were smoked in a rabbit hole!

All in all, it was an incredibly happy, carefree time – at least for us kids. We were really active kids. How could we not be, when we were surrounded by a huge, empty playground, begging to be explored? We were usually filthy because it was impossible to keep clean; staying clean was quite the challenge. To bath, if that's what you'd call it, we would use a 'stacker', the plastic storage bin in which we'd keep our camp oven and those types of things. Just as the sun was going down, before we'd leave the camp, Mum would boil the billy over the fire and pour the water into the stacker, and then call us in for 'the wash'.

I was small enough to sit inside the stacker, which was like a bath. Water was rationed, it was the most precious thing we had – the worst thing we kids could do was to waste a drop of water

– so Mum would wash me and Nash first, and then she and Dad would use the same water, bathing in the leftovers. Sometimes we were forced to wash our hair in cattle troughs. Clean-ish troughs, of course. Other times we'd use artesian bores, where the water was a bit cleaner.

We dined well on the kangaroo, rabbits, wild turkey, wild duck, emu and pigeon we caught (our Seventh Day Adventist vegetarian beliefs went out of the window pretty quickly in the outback), and we ate tinned food like Fray Bentos pies, which I still love, the rest of the time. We gorged on bread baked by Mum in a camp oven and drank rationed water, boiled before drinking. On special occasions we'd share a can of ginger beer, which we regarded as a huge treat. And a few times a year with our cousins, Narelle, Traci and Clint, Nash and I would put on a little play performance.

We were deadly serious about these plays. For a week beforehand there were rehearsals, where we worked out our parts, and dressed up in our parents' clothes and also tried to think what to do with Clint who was really young and didn't follow directions well. We performed our versions of stories we knew; once it was 'The Tortoise and the Hare' and another time we staged a version of a Sherlock Holmes mystery with Nash as Holmes and me as Doctor Watson. We'd charge our parents ten cents each; after all, how much entertainment did they get out there? There was an improvised stage – or sometimes we'd cut the bottom out of a cardboard box and pretend it was a television. Then we'd squeeze inside the box and read out the news.

The ten cents 'cover charge' from our plays was used to buy a treat from the Special Train, which went through the Nullarbor twice a year. There were a few of these trains, most of them supplying food and other essentials to the families who were working on the railroads and who lived in the sidings. One was the Tea and Sugar Train; this was like a little IGA on wheels that came through every fortnight. The Special Train, though, had the good stuff – toy carriages – where we were allowed to buy one toy each. I vividly recall Nash buying a tomahawk. I bought a truck. A Coke truck with a trailer and a racing car on the back. I still have it today and both my boys love playing with it.

One experience sticks in my mind and I've always wanted to relate it because it says a lot about the incredible generosity of the few people we did encounter out in the desert. Mum and I were on the Tea and Sugar Train searching for a dummy for my doll, which was one of the few 'proper' toys I kept with me out there. There was no way in the world we were going to find a doll's dummy on the Tea and Sugar train, of course, because it was mainly for supplies, but this old man on the train overheard us. He told me he had a granddaughter who was about my age and that he knew exactly the right dummy that I needed. He even promised that he'd send it to me.

This just seemed too unlikely for words, of course, and Mum clearly thought, 'Well, we're never going to hear from him again.' But I truly believed him; I guess I had no reason not to at that age, and I told Mum that I knew he would be true to his word. She must have been thinking, 'Poor, deluded girl.' But sure enough, a few weeks later the promised dummy turned up in a parcel at the roadhouse where we collected our mail, along with a copy of the book *The Water Babies*, which I still have. I also kept the note that he wrote, which simply said: 'From your friend on the train.'

Some of the experiences we had out there on the Nullarbor were so bizarre that even now they're still hard to believe. In July 1979, when I was barely three, a hefty chunk of the space station *Skylab* crashed to earth, and just so happened to land about 60 kilometres from where we were camped. The beautiful solitude and silence of the Nullarbor – *our* Nullarbor – was shattered. There were people and cars everywhere; we didn't know what the hell had happened until someone told us, and even then we had to ask what *Skylab* actually was. Our only source of news was the occasional newspaper that would be thrown to us from a passing train, which would be a few weeks old when we read them. And we were really too absorbed in our own private world to be too interested in the rest of the planet.

There was a strange, surreal quality to the Nullarbor sometimes. Whenever there was a torrential rain, quite a rare thing, wildflowers would somehow emerge through this dry, barren earth and spring up all over the place. I'd wake up and feel as though I'd emerged, like Alice, on the other side of the looking glass: this just couldn't be real. The landscape that only a few days before had been red and parched and pretty much dead was now alive with colour. Wildflowers would spring up literally everywhere – it was this mad explosion of colour: pink, white, yellow, red flowers, in all directions. Like I said, it didn't happen often, but when it did we felt like kids in a huge, vivid playground.

And if Dad was still a church-going man, he'd swear on a stack of Bibles that he once woke to see an Afghani, in full traditional costume, and a camel train, making their way across the Nullarbor. The Afghani had some women with him, his harem, I guess, all seated on camels. The guy simply looked over at our camp, acknowledged Dad, and kept moving. He didn't even stop for a chat. I mean, he's leading camels across the Nullarbor and probably hasn't seen a person for months, and he just kept walking. Dad still wonders if he was hallucinating. He told me that he rubbed his eyes in amazement and thought: 'I'm going mad. This outback life has finally caught up with me and I'm going crazy.'

In many ways, we drew a lot from the Aboriginal way of life. I really did feel, and still do feel, a strong connection with Aborigines living off the land, just as we were doing on the Nullarbor. As a child, my great-grandfather, Stan Chambers, said he remembered an Aboriginal named Lanky who said he worked for the Chambers family years ago. Lanky was the last remaining member of the Buandik tribe who lived in the area. Grandpa recalled a lot of survival stories as told by Lanky. There's a water hole called 'Lanky's Well' in Beachport named in his honour.

Dad always made it clear to us that we, too, were living the Aboriginal way, and that we should have respect and appreciation for that. We encountered as many Aborigines as we did white people, perhaps even more, while living on the Nullarbor. The Chambers clan was acknowledged by Southend locals as being very much in tune with the Aboriginal approach to life. That fascination lives on today in my eldest son, Tal, who is besotted by anything to do with Indigenous culture, so it seems to be something that has stayed strong throughout many generations of my family.

'Mum,' Tal once told me, 'when I grow up, I want to be an Aborigine. Okay?'

An exciting thing for Nash and me while out on the Nullarbor was searching for Aboriginal spearheads. But I'd get a little over-excited; often I'd pick up some rock, basically nothing, and run around insisting that it was a spearhead. Nash would take one look and burst my bubble. 'That's not a spearhead,' he'd say, and throw it away. But we would find a lot of them, which we'd always hang onto.

One time we found a traditional boomerang, obviously one that didn't come back! It's now hanging on the wall of Nash's home studio.

Later on, when we were touring in the Dead Ringer Band, we'd head into places such as Coober Pedy and Alice Springs, and the majority of our audience would be Aboriginal, many of whom loved country music and seemed to really relate to us.

I sometimes felt bored out on the Nullarbor, but it was always a temporary, transitory experience: I might have been bored by our camp, or bored by the rain, which meant that we were stuck inside the car for the day, or were holed up in the trailer playing Boggle and Uno, games like that – but I was never bored by the experience of being out in the desert.

I'd sometimes write letters and send them to our family back in Southend, updating them on what was happening in our lives.

Dear Nanna and Pa,

Hi. How are you? We are well up here. Nash got a bow and 16 arrows; 12 were not made up and four were. He shot four rabbits and hit seven, but didn't see the seven rabbits.

Luv from Kasey

Shooting rabbits, bows and arrows – it was just another day in our outback paradise, apparently!

These days, my family understand that fox hunting isn't the most politically correct way of making a living. And it does seem strange in some ways – Dad is such a gentle man and yet here he was, making a living from killing things.

The truth is that in rural areas there was, and is, a different attitude towards hunting and a different view of foxes and rabbits – they were known as pests and needed to be kept in check. Plus, strange as it may sound, Mum and Dad abided by certain codes of conduct; poisoned baits, for instance, were frowned upon because they were a danger to all animals, not just foxes. Some hunters used strychnine, while others used cyanide, which was more deadly. A heavy rain could wash away cyanide, but strychnine would continue through the food chain – so if a fox ate a bait and a dingo ate the fox, they'd both die, and so on.

If Nash or I found a bait, we knew it was best to tell our parents and not touch it. The indiscriminate killing could extend to humans as well; Gary Chambers, Dad's cousin, once leant down to look at a bait, the wind changed and blew the fumes his way, and he was crook for days to the point where Val, his wife, thought he might die.

But there's also an argument against hunting animals for fur and eventually the conservation movement caught up with the Nullarbor. After about eight years the market for fox skins began to fade as fur coats fell out of fashion. By the mid-1980s, the healthy living Dad made from fox hunting dropped off and he started hunting rabbits instead, which didn't pay as well.

By 1986, other things were changing. I was ten years old, Nash was set to begin high school, and Mum wasn't sure she was up to the demands of continuing his education by correspondence. She wanted us to get a social education, too. I think she worried that all that time out in the outback by ourselves might turn us into loners (in Nash's case she may have left it too late – he's always happier away from people!). And aside from that, I think my parents were ready for a change. Perhaps they needed some privacy and space after all those years of living in a car with Nash and me.

Ten years of living out there does take a toll – though, by the end, things had become a little easier in some ways. We had a chiller for storing the rabbits and we also used it for keeping food cold, an unheard-of luxury before then – we even had a little VCR and TV. Nanna would fill tapes with my two favourite shows, *Diff'rent Strokes* and *Webster*, which she'd post to us, and we'd watch them repeatedly.

My love of sitcoms – I've spent countless nights falling asleep to tapes of *Seinfeld*, *The King of Queens* and *Friends* and can recite entire episodes from memory – can be traced back to then. We had one movie on tape: *Lone Wolf McQuade*, with Chuck Norris. That was the only thing we had and we watched it every single day for three months until Nanna sent out something else. I named a pet rabbit McQuade, in honour of Chuck. Yet, despite these little creature comforts, it was still a wearing life.

There was no big announcement about not heading out to the Nullarbor again. More likely someone said, 'I don't think we'll go out next season.' Nash went out with Dad a few more times – never for a season, just short trips. I didn't go back again. But even though years have passed, that time stays with me.

Today, when I hear someone speak about the Nullarbor, I react with pride. It was one of the most exciting and unforgettable stages of my life. You know when someone talks about your home town? That's what it feels like to me. I feel even more strongly about the Nullarbor than I do about Southend, as much as I loved most of my life there. Not many people can call the Nullarbor their home, their backyard. I now feel like some kind of ambassador for the place!

I have one last story which sums up the place for me. During our final year of being hunters, we were on the property of a man called Bobby Hunter, a lovely guy, who lived alone, about 500 kilometres northeast of the Nullarbor, at Stuart Creek out on the Oodnadatta track. He let us hunt on his station. We'd been there for a few weeks, perhaps even months, and we were getting ready to go back to Southend for good. We said our goodbyes to Bobby, who then went out to look after his cattle, but before we left, it started to rain. Mum, being everyone's mother, went out and took Bobby's washing off the clothesline for him and left it inside his house. Then we drove home.

About ten years later, we were playing a gig at the Maree Camel Cup, and we spotted him in the crowd. 'Wow, look, it's Bobby Hunter,' we said, truly thrilled to see him again. We went over and re-introduced ourselves, he looked at us, and just as if it had been yesterday, said, matter-of-factly, 'Hey, thanks for bringing my washing in.'

2

Southend

I grew up a long way from here
I slept with the lights on for fifteen years
And Sabbath kept me home on Friday nights
And Daddy sang me Rodgers
Just to make everything all right.

Lyrics from 'Southern Kind of Life'

I'd say around 200 people lived in Southend in 1976 when I was born, and many of them had the same surname as me. Five generations back, Dad's Swedish ancestor, Jacob 'Jake' Chambers, had decided to settle in the nearby coastal town of Robe (he was on a ship bound for Melbourne but on a trip ashore he spotted the local barmaid, liked the look of her and decided to stay). Since then that area of SA has been home to people called Chambers.

Dad's father and mother, who I call Poppa Jake and Nanna Judy, raised their seven children in Southend. There were four boys – Bill, Leigh, Jarrod and Barry, who, tragically, was lost at sea when I was quite young – and three girls: Julie, Keryn and Jeanie.

All the siblings except Dad married locals and settled around the same area. Dad's brothers all became fishermen; his sisters married fishermen. So when we were in Southend, we really lived that saying 'It takes a village to raise a child'; all the Chambers raised all the Chambers children. We went drainfishing with our cousins, ate with our uncles and aunts. And we sang along with them after dinner or at church or Bible studies or during a barbecue. Music was another of my constants.

Southend is basically a fishing village. It sits at one end of a 6-kilometre-long bay, with the town of Beachport at the other end. In Beachport you'll find a pub and a couple of restaurants – that's the place a lot of tourists from Adelaide or other surrounding towns go for their summer holidays and it has a population of around 500 people.

Our town was small enough that there was no need for a traffic light or even a stop sign. If we wanted to give people directions to our house, we'd simply tell them, 'It's the first house on the right.'

Once we were off the Nullarbor and back in Southend for good, we settled into a more regular existence, living in the beach shack my parents had bought for $7000. It was a three-bedroom weatherboard shanty that could have blown over in a strong wind. Nash and I were enrolled in school in nearby Rendelsham, and during my first week at school I cried every day at the thought of being separated from Mum.

After the nothingness of the Nullarbor, Southend felt like a bustling metropolis to me. People, mostly relatives, popped in and out of our house – no need to call beforehand as you might now – after all, where else could you be? Mum and Dad seemed to be making up for all those isolated years with their new zeal for family gatherings and barbecues. And I slotted back in with the friends I'd made over the years of going back and forth.

Most of the extended Chambers are typical rural Australians in one sense; they grow their own food and they know how to hunt and shoot. My Poppa Jake would sometimes head out to the Nullarbor, a good two days' drive away, and live out there for a month, using the survival skills he'd pass onto his kids. In Poppa and Nanna's house, a kangaroo carcass hanging from the ceiling is not an unusual occurrence – I didn't think about it until years later when a non-Southend friend came over and reeled back a bit at the sight.

As I said earlier, the Chambers clan (and all of my immediate family too, for a while) were Seventh Day Adventists. Nanna and Poppa were both the most welcoming, warm-hearted people you could meet, so this wasn't religion in the strict and judgmental sense, but there was always a Bible open at their place and both of them would quote from it. When we left the house, Nanna would say things like 'God will protect you', 'Talk to the Lord if you're in trouble'; that type of thing. Poppa Jake is different. He looks like an old-style bush prophet, with his long beard and bushie's clothes, and in some ways that's what he is.

Dad remembers once playing a solo gig in the local beer garden at Southend. Poppa Jake was in the audience, along with a lot of

Dad's family, and Dad suggested they sing one together, which was a regular occurrence if Poppa was at a show.

'Bill, I don't need you for this,' Poppa Jake said. 'You can sit down.'

Dad did as he was told, reluctantly; after all, it was his show, a sold-out gig at that. Poppa crossed his hands, as if he was about to sing a hymn. But first he had an announcement to make:

'About a month ago, I was passing blood in my urine,' he told a stunned crowd. 'So I went to the doctor and all he did was stuff his finger up my bum.'

Dad and his sisters were in stitches. They were half expecting something odd or religious, but they weren't expecting this. Poppa told this long story about what the doctor did to him and in the end said, 'But I have healed myself. All I had to do was have faith in God.' And then, finally, he sang the gospel song, 'The Old Rugged Cross', just a verse, and sat back down. My Nanna was under the table, dying of embarrassment. But that's what he's like. He doesn't consider who's in the room or whether it's appropriate; if he's in the mood, he's going to preach, and sometimes that 'preachy' mood can last for months.

Poppa Jake is also a keen hunter. I once called him and said that I was bringing a friend and wanted to do some hunting.

'Are there any foxes around?' I asked.

He said no, but told me there might be a few rabbits.

But as we were driving into Southend, we passed a wombat road sign and we saw a fox run across the road. When we arrived,

I said to Poppa that I saw a fox. He asked me where; when I told him he said, 'Which way was he headed?'

I told him and he looked at me, deadly serious, and said, 'I know him.'

And I believed him. Why wouldn't I?

Around the age of 11, not too long after we returned from the Nullarbor, I began to experience night terrors, and everyone around me quickly came to understand why they're called 'terrors'. It was horrible. I now realise that my terrors were connected to an incident one time when I was staying overnight at a friend's house and awoke to find a distant relative of my friend, who was also staying in the house, attempting to touch me inappropriately.

My night terrors started not long after that horrible experience – an experience I didn't share with anyone, my parents included, until years later, hoping it might somehow disappear from my memory. In my night terrors, strangely, I didn't dream about what went on that night. I can't recall exactly what I was dreaming about, but I do know I wasn't reliving anything.

I figured that if I made a big deal of it, it would then become a big deal to me. I so badly wanted the entire experience to disappear that I convinced myself that I was over-reacting and it was merely part of a 'stupid little playtime' that I didn't understand because I was just a kid. And part of me just didn't want to cause trouble which I knew would erupt if I told anyone about this night. I was also confused about how to bring it up with anyone

– because, how do you discuss such a thing? What words could I use to describe something so invasive, so confusing? Merely thinking about it made me uncomfortable, let alone talking it through with anyone, no matter how well I knew them, or how much I trusted them.

In hindsight, I think I was more affected by the whole thing later in life, when I was old enough to understand what had happened. At the time, my day-to-day life was unchanged – I was still a happy-go-lucky kid. I didn't say a word to my parents or to Nash or to friends, but I did once refer to it a bit cryptically in a school essay. We'd been reading *The Colour Purple* at the time – Alice Walker's book that talks about the sexual abuse of a young girl – and it clearly struck a chord with me. My teacher, Mr Stanbridge, was quick to pick up the reference and he pulled me aside after class to say, 'If there's ever anything you want to talk about, Kasey, just come to me, okay?' I liked and respected this teacher but I was so embarrassed I just said 'Yeah, sure' and ran off.

Aside from that, I largely left it alone. In my teens I revealed small details to boyfriends whose attempts at getting too intimate had me backing off. It didn't help those relationships, and it wasn't an effective way of dealing with it for me, but it was all I had for a long time. I'd go for months without even thinking about what went on that night. I wasn't some sad, damaged kid like you'd see in movies. I simply pushed it away. What happened in my mind while I was asleep, however, was a different thing: that was something I couldn't control.

So I started to develop night terrors in my sleep. For anyone who hasn't witnessed or experienced these sleep disorders, let me just say that the word 'terror' isn't too strong a description – they are well beyond nightmares, a deeply frightening experience for everyone involved, and they still affect me today though far less often.

The night terrors started to come on quickly when I was 11 years old. One night I went to sleep and some hours later it was as if I'd woken up, but I hadn't. I began screaming hysterically. Mum and Dad bolted into my room; they had no idea what was going on, or exactly what to do.

The feeling that I had, that I can recall, was even scarier than the experience itself. It was pure, primal fear, as if I knew someone had broken into the house and was coming to kill me. It was a feeling without real definition – part of the trouble is that in the mornings after I'd had one of these attacks, I would wake up feeling that something was off, but I had no memory of what. But for the people who were awake it was completely unnerving; I'd get out of bed and run around the house, just screaming. I'd even be scared of my parents; I'd look at them, apparently, but not see them.

Once they started, the night terrors became horribly regular. God knows what the neighbours were thinking; what was going on in the Chambers house? I soon became scared of going to sleep. I'd wake up really exhausted, and the same goes for my parents, I'm sure.

Mum admits that she didn't know how to react. They'd try and calm me down, which was the natural reaction, but I just didn't acknowledge them. They wanted to comfort me, but after a few attacks they realised that I wasn't totally there. At first they'd try and wake me up, which as it turns out isn't the best thing to do, and I would become even more hysterical. When I did wake up I'd be so scared – I didn't really know what I was scared of, exactly – but after a time I'd slowly settle down and let Mum and Dad comfort me.

For a long time I wasn't allowed to have sleepovers with friends, because it just wasn't fair on the other parents if I had an attack. That may not seem like a big deal now but at 11 sleepovers were a huge part of my world – and I really felt I was missing out on something. My parents even had to install a key-operated lock on our front door, because during an attack I would try and get outside the house. And this was in Southend, where no one locked their doors. Mum said she feared I was acting like someone who was possessed. As for me, I thought I was some kind of weirdo, a freak.

My parents took me to see a few different doctors, without any real improvement. One doctor thought I was suffering a form of epilepsy. I don't recall anyone identifying my problem as 'night terrors' – maybe the term wasn't in use back then, although it's now recognised as a natural sleep disorder.

But the last person that Mum and Dad took me to see had a different approach. I was 13 by then and typically the doctors would look me over and talk with me and then speak separately with Mum and Dad, but in this case the doctor spoke with all of us. He said, 'I think what she's doing is bottling up any problems or negative feelings she is experiencing, and they come out during her sleep.' That made perfect sense to me, and for different reasons, it made sense to my parents. From that night onwards these night terrors stopped occurring regularly. It was as if I'd solved the problem, because I now understood what was happening to me.

The doctor did help ease the frequency of my night terrors, but just when I thought it was safe to go back to sleep, I started sleepwalking. In some ways that was just as bad for me – I still wasn't allowed to have sleepovers, and they were the most important things in the world to a kid my age! At some point in the night I'd simply get up and wander around the house. Mum and Dad would talk to me, thinking I was awake, but it didn't take them long to work out what was going on.

I once sleepwalked into Nash's room, while he was there with some of his friends. In a typical teenager's way, he said: 'What are you doing? Get out.' I began to have this conversation with him that made no sense at all. Then I walked out and did exactly the same with Mum and Dad. It was all a little crazy. Mum was told by a doctor not to wake me up; that was the worse thing she could do. So she'd just coolly walk me to bed, saying stuff like: 'Come on, let's go back to sleep now.'

The question which still haunts me is, of course, why did this happen? Did it have anything to do with what had happened at my girlfriend's place? I'm not a psychologist – watching a lot of Oprah and Dr Phil doesn't give you a qualification – but in my head one was a trigger for the other. I might have been prone to night terrors and sleepwalking anyway. It didn't help though that I had a habit – even back then – of shelving anything that I find too hard to deal with.

I don't mean to make it sound as if coming back to Southend was the end of the good times; there were plenty of fun things happening in my life then too. For a start, Mum and Dad had taken up their musical careers again and this time Nash and I were part of the band – sort of.

I'm not sure that the band – which we called the Dead Ringer Band, as all our family look alike – was entirely serious. Dad was ambitious, but not in a 'success at all costs way', he just loved playing and he loved all of us playing together. Mum always enjoyed music, though she probably wouldn't have been so involved if she hadn't met Dad who taught her how to play bass and got her up on stage.

As a kid, Dad leaned towards the music coming off his parents' gramophone, country music made by the Carter Family and later Johnny Cash and Hank Williams. He loves music that is powerful and has a dangerous sound to it, all those stories of hard living and heartache and loneliness (he is allergic to anything too perky, shiny and happy in music). As a young man, he got into folk and also Brit pop and rock; Dylan, the Stones, the Beatles as well as The Byrds and Gram Parsons. On the surface those artists belong in different genres but musically they were all speaking to each other. There are certain blends in all of Dad's – and my – favourite music where you can hear a kind of history coming through.

Dad taught himself guitar by imitating the chords he heard on his parents' 78s. And he had his look early on too; in photos of him from the 1970s he looks how you'd imagine a folk singer from San Francisco might appear, with his shoulder-length hair and beard, mellow smile and slight hippy vibe. He looked like a young Jackson Browne. (Although I thought he looked a little like Jesus Christ, frankly. I would glance at him sometimes and think, 'Well, who knows, maybe …')

Though everyone in the family sang and played music and Poppa Jake even wrote his own songs, Dad was the one who took it the furthest. In the 1960s he played with a local group called The Ramblers, which included Mum's cousin 'Flogger' Dean, who actually introduced Mum and Dad. The story is on the night they met Dad asked Mum what music she loved. 'Johnny Cash and Bob Dylan,' she replied. Dad smiled and thought to himself: 'I'm gonna marry you.'

Mum was born in Melbourne, but when her parents split up she went to live with her mother and stepfather, Margaret and Bill Walker, in Mannum on the Murray River near Adelaide and about four or five hours drive from Southend. Because we lived in a town full of Chambers, I know Dad's family better than Mum's;

hers was the 'treat' family we went to visit on holidays. From what I know of Mum in her younger days, she was a little rebellious, hanging out with what would have been gangs and dreaming of joining the Navy. I guess that restlessness gave her something in common with Dad, but in other ways they are opposites; Dad is dreamy, unaware of the world around him; Mum is very perceptive, sensitive to people's moods, a fixer and an organiser. I've inherited traits from both – and I've certainly inherited their love of socialising; all of us are world-class talkers.

After they met, Dad had his own band, The Deerstalkers, and made a few TV appearances. The band played at dances and school formals, and in pubs. Shortly before they married, in 1970 – they fast-tracked their wedding so Dad, who was very anti-war, could avoid National Service to Vietnam – they made their live debut as a duo, playing at a joint called Old Gus's Tavern. It was in Andamooka, an opal-mining town about 600 ks north of Adelaide, where a crowd of around 20 people cheered them on, including one guy who was so drunk he couldn't stand up. They did pretty well in the early 1970s, too, playing in and around a part of the south called the Green Triangle, which spanned the border area between South Australia and Victoria. They sang covers and also original songs that Dad wrote.

Pretty soon after returning to Southend from the outback, they started playing again. They were joined by two friends: Robert Leslie, who was a great singer and songwriter, and Colin Potter – a sax player, of all things, in this country band – who spoke with a strong Scottish brogue. Nash occasionally starred on drums or played guitar. They would sing favourite songs from the Eagles or Creedence Clearwater Revival or Johnny Cash – and some original songs by Robert.

I was especially fond of Robert. For a time I had a crush on one of his six sons, a boy named Scott. I'd tell Mum and Dad that I was going to visit my grandparents, who lived in Rendelsham, but I would actually go and see Scott. I always looked forward to his father's visits; he was such a terrific guy. Robert was an Aussie, also of Scottish descent, and he had that distinctly Scottish sense of humour, which I loved.

Mum and Dad were still actively involved with the church, even if their faith in their faith had started to slide a little. But it gave Dad a further chance to get back into music. We'd go to services on Saturday and on Friday nights we'd host Bible groups, or visit the homes of others from the church.

The adults would do Bible readings, Dad would play some gospel songs, while we'd go off and play. Dad told me that it was a long time before he was allowed to bring a guitar into church. The guitar was the work of the devil; church was all about singing and playing the organ. We were vegetarians for a while, too, in keeping with the beliefs of the Adventists, although Nash and I would sometimes sneak off to a shop in Southend and he would buy meat with his 'lolly money'. He'd buy what we called a 'fritz', which was like devon, processed meat, something we weren't allowed to eat at home. I, of course, bought lollies!

But what I recall most strongly about these gatherings was the idea of 'cool, we get to play with other kids'. I respected the idea of religion and God but I really just wanted to hang out.

I had good friends, especially Caddie Ellis. Caddie enjoyed those Friday night get-togethers, especially singing gospel songs, so she and I would spend a lot of time with each other, much of it at our house. Caddie was one of three sisters, born within three years of each other, and our mothers were very close. Caddie and I started to grow even closer when we got to sing together with the Dead Ringers.

We had a caravan parked at the front of our house, which was connected to the main house by a hole that Dad cut in the wall. Mum and Dad slept in the van, which gave them the room to set up and rehearse inside the house. Band practice, which took place in our living room, was a highlight of the week for me. It was exciting, not least because Caddie and I persuaded the band to let us sing occasionally. Our idea of songs at that stage were the themes of our favourite TV shows like *Charles in Charge* – 'Charles in charge / of our days and our nights' – and *Punky Brewster*. I can still sing that today, word for word. ('Maybe the world is blind / Or just a little unkind.') Ah, the memories.

Often, if the band was taking a break, Caddie and I would ask Dad to leave the microphone on and we'd get up and have a sing, just the two of us. So it seemed sort of inevitable that we'd graduate to singing with the band in front of an audience.

Southend's club was the scene of our big debut. Usually the band played on the pavement in neighbouring Beachport – outside the fresh fish shop my parents had bought and were running by then. Beachport gets the summer tourist trade so the strip outside the shop got quite a few pedestrians walking past and eventually the band was playing there once a fortnight. We had the publicity angle all stitched up: a few days before each gig we'd stick a notice in the window of the local fish and chip shop. Simple.

The Southend club is a really small hall, with a tiny bar and a couple of pool tables. It's more like a rec room, but with a licence. Dad had suggested that Caddie and I learn a few songs to sing on the night and we'd ditched our TV themes for a couple of big radio hits from the time: Cyndi Lauper's 'Time After Time' and Dire Straits's 'Walk of Life'. We didn't have much of a stage act; we were so nervous that we barely moved. We were like statues. It was scary as hell – completely different to school productions, which I'd been involved with and found pretty easy, or rehearsals. To sing in front of other people, who were staring at us, and who we knew, was another thing altogether. I don't think Caddie and I even looked at each other while we were singing, we were that concerned about putting each other off.

However, we really liked it. Enough to do it again. Okay, we were completely stoked; it was such a kick to sing live, even though we couldn't bring ourselves to speak in between the songs yet. All chuffed up, we entered a local talent quest at Millicent School, where we sang the Bangles' big hit, 'Manic Monday' and learned our first hard lesson about the music industry: there's no such thing as an overnight success. I think we might have won a place but the winner was Helen Sanderson, a ballerina.

After that we started doing a few live gigs with the Dead Ringers, where we'd sing two or three songs, and then that expanded into five, maybe six songs. We wouldn't be on stage all night; Mum and Dad would tell us when our 'bracket' was, we'd come out, do our thing, and then go and hang out backstage – when there was a stage.

It was acceptable for young kids to be at the gigs, even though they were in pubs. South Australia didn't have pokies so the pubs we played at were mostly places where families went for dinner. Kids from school would come along with their parents. The band got gigs in several surrounding areas and more often than not Caddie and I were there, perfecting our sets.

Caddie and I would bring all our toys, pencils and paper and sleeping stuff to the gigs, to fill in the time we weren't on stage. These were long gigs, running four or five hours until the early morning, and by the time the band finished we'd be fast asleep, curled up behind the amps. Mum and Dad would pour us into the car and we'd snooze all the way home.

I'd been a bit of a tomboy out in the outback, and there wasn't much occasion to dress up in Southend. The band though, gave me an excuse to develop my new interest in fashion. From the start I wanted to look different. There were a lot of girl bands and female singers on the charts then – Tiffany, Belinda Carlisle,

Debbie Gibson – and then there was Cyndi Lauper, the quirky girl. I wanted to be Cyndi – not just in terms of clothes, but how she sang and the songs she picked, which weren't the usual bubblegum; the fact that she had her own style. Caddie didn't much mind either way but she followed my directions when I suggested we pair our rah-rah skirts with boots and a hat.

Caddie and I also started getting paid for singing, which was great. We'd all get a free meal and our share of the take was $12.50 each per gig, most of which I spent on cassette tapes. We started broadening our sets into a mix of contemporary stuff, then something by Emmylou Harris or Nicolette Larson's 'That's More About Love'. We'd try Roseanne Cash songs, and Johnny Cash, too. Even Merle Haggard. Gradually, we settled into a routine where Caddie would sing the harmony parts, and I'd sing the lead. We didn't actually know what singing harmony meant; it just happened by chance one day while we were singing together. The irony was that Caddie is a more naturally talented singer than me – I couldn't harmonise to save my life, but it came easily to her – but because I took the lead she was pushed into the background a little.

Though it started to feel more natural for me to be on stage, I still couldn't bring myself to speak to the audience. Dad would do all that. He'd say, 'Caddie and Kasey are now going to sing this song by Emmylou Harris' and off we'd go. In order to give me something to do on stage, he suggested that I hold an acoustic guitar – I didn't have to plug it in which was good because the thought of playing guitar live was slightly more terrifying than talking – but I could get my confidence up by playing air guitar, though on a real instrument. It really was the best way to learn, although I've never developed much as a guitarist.

There weren't a lot of bands coming out to do gigs around the Southend area, so the Dead Ringers got lots of bookings playing weddings, 21st birthdays, stuff like that. Oh my God, if I had a dollar for every time I sang 'The Power of Love' as a freaking bridal waltz, I'd be one very wealthy woman! I realise that it's a big moment for newlyweds, but there's something ridiculous about being serenaded by a 12-year-old. Anyway, we started to become a little popular and were known locally as the country band that everyone would hire. We'd play two shows most weekends, which was pretty good, considering where we were and the fact that Nash and I were beginners.

We tried to be crowd pleasers, but we occasionally veered off into more interesting territory. The people who came to see us would have been happy for us to play anything, because we were a local family, but they had their favourites. They'd go wild for Johnny Cash's 'Folsom Prison Blues'. Then we'd throw in a bit of rugged country rock by hard man Steve Earle or something folksy from Nanci Griffith and they'd love it, but if you played that stuff all night, well, things could get tricky.

Playing music for an audience did some good things for my self-esteem, which wasn't in the best of shape back then, because of the trouble I was having adapting to 'regular' school, and my night terrors. The fact that I was in a band gave me a kind of status and I don't remember anyone teasing me about being 'country' though it wasn't hip even back then. I got to go to a pub every Friday or Saturday night with my best friend, we got paid – and people came to hear us sing. It felt great. When I was singing I thought I was the coolest person in the world. Well, at least the coolest kid in Southend.

3

'Do I know you?'

So before you disappear again
Just think of what you're feeling and don't go
There's more to what you're telling me
I'm not buying what you're selling me – don't go.

Lyrics from 'Don't Go'

As Dad's family had always been in the fishing business, it seemed natural, once we were settled back in Southend, for he and Mum to set up a fresh fish shop – called The Trawl Net – in Beachport. If you've ever seen the Aussie film, *Sweet Talker*, which starred Bryan Brown and Karen Allen – don't worry, not too many people saw it when it came out, or since – the shop and our family car feature there. You might even be able to pick us out in the crowd scenes; the whole town made sure they got in those. When the film crew came to town and shot their movie it was one of the biggest things to happen to Beachport.

Many of the cast and crew would hang out in the local pub at Beachport and the Dead Ringer Band played there every night during the shoot. Karen Allen – who's best known for racing around with Harrison Ford in *Raiders of the Lost Ark* – even got up and sang with us once. She could hold a tune, too. On another night Bryan Brown got behind the bar and started spinning bottles, re-enacting his role in the film *Cocktail*. It was all pretty impressive for a small community. The town was absolutely alive.

During the shooting of the film, Rachel Ward, Bryan Brown's wife, came in to buy some mussels, which we had to order for her. Dad had a major crush on Rachel – and fair enough, too; she's a beautiful, classy woman. Eventually her order of mussels turned up but Rachel didn't. Yet Dad refused to sell them just in case Rachel returned: he was that smitten by her. Finally, the crew had gone, the film was over, everything was finished, the town was back to its sleepy self, but Dad still kept Rachel's mussels, just in case. About six months passed before we convinced him that she was truly gone. Broke his heart.

I worked behind the counter at our shop after school. It was the first 'real' job that I ever had. We sold lots of different fish: deep-sea fish, even some shark, all bought from the fishing boats that docked at the jetty directly across from our shop. I'd serve some customers, but mainly did the shitty jobs because I was the newbie. I would fillet fish, gut them, cut off their heads; it didn't bother me what job I was asked to do, with one exception. I hated 'horning' crayfish, which meant I had to break off the horns. Those you would sell separately; some people considered that the best meat. But that's the spikiest part of the crayfish and I'd end up with spikes all over my hands. It was a horrible job. Mum and Dad were lenient with me; they'd usually let me knock off early and hang out with all the local kids in the upstairs room which had become a drop-in centre.

Soon after Mum and Dad opened the fish shop in Beachport I met the person who would become my unlikely best friend and soul mate; Steven 'Worm' Werchon. I'm not sure how to describe Worm, as he's known to everyone. Physically, he looks like someone you'd avoid on a dark street, short and stocky, with tattoos and piercings. When we met he was 14, two years older than me, and he had a reputation as a wild child, a bit of a long-haired hoon around town. Nash, who was a bit bolshie himself, actually warned me off him once, saying, 'And I don't want to see you hanging around with that fucking Worm!'

If I've learned anything about myself it's that I'm magnetically drawn to people like Worm who I feel are misunderstood and just need me to 'fix' them and reveal their good side to the world. I've been proven wrong more than once, but in Worm's case, my faith paid off. Underneath his tough exterior, he is not just a softy, but utterly loyal and likeable, one of the rare people with whom I can be myself. Yes, he looks like he could eat children, but in reality, he is hilariously scared of spiders and horror movies.

There was no great romance between me and Worm, though we did share a moment. A moment he doesn't actually remember. It happened at a party in Beachport when I found myself sitting next to Worm, and out of the blue he turned around and started kissing me. I was shocked: 'Oh my God, Worm's kissing me, I know this guy! I can't believe he's noticed me.' I was so young and clueless I figured we were now a couple. We'd kissed, so we were as good as married. Right?

The next day I saw Worm, out on the jetty, across from Mum and Dad's shop – I was sitting there, looking out the window, hoping that he would walk past – and I ran outside and tapped him on the shoulder. 'Hello,' I said to him, and then asked, 'So, you know, what did last night mean for us now?' He looked at me oddly and asked: 'Do I know you?' He'd been so drunk that night that he kissed everyone, including a long-haired boy he'd mistaken for a girl; he just didn't remember me at all.

We did date on and off for a while but our relationship blossomed into friendship and then into a brother-sister bond. I was barely old enough for serious romance anyway, and we mostly hung out a lot together. I had a lot of girl friends at school but my after-school pals were boys like Worm and his two pals, Mitch and Jamie. Why? I don't know. Girls are just more complicated.

Looking back on my adolescence I feel incredibly lucky to have had the parents I did. They were caring but not strict, open to anything I wanted to lay on their laps, tolerant of the troubled kids I hung out with. They would have needed every ounce of that tolerance because teenage rebellion hit me with a vengeance.

I wasn't a really bad teenager, or a really sour one, I was just lost. I felt all wrong, both as though I knew everything and as if I knew nothing at all. Nash, who had been more of a handful as a kid, almost swapped roles with me at that point; suddenly I was the difficult one while he seemed more sure of himself. But maybe it always feels like that.

What I know is that almost overnight I started acting like someone from an American teen movie: smoking, skipping school, feeling resentful towards the teachers. I didn't enjoy school and after all my years of freedom on the Nullarbor I couldn't get used to the long hours and the structure and the feeling of being no good at anything. I'll admit I had a defeatist attitude – the Chambers family, including Dad, had a less-than-excellent academic history; none of us had made it to college. I didn't feel I belonged at school. So instead I'd give it a miss and go hang out with a bunch of kids called the Waggers group, many of whom were far more lost than me. So in that sense I wasn't alienated from everyone; the confusion was inside my own head.

Drama class was the exception. I'd loved drama since primary school. Even though I was only in class for a couple of months each year before returning to the Nullarbor, I'd scored the lead roles in a few end-of-year productions, which were staged for parents, teachers and family at the Rendelsham Hall. I usually got the parts because there was some singing involved: I was Snow White and also played Joseph in *Joseph and the Amazing Technicolour Dreamcoat*. The school's principal, Mr Gabb, was one of the teachers that would select me for these lead roles. He was among the few teachers that I connected with, along with John McKinnon.

I saw Mr Gabb years later when he came out to one of our gigs down south. I wondered if he was proud of me, an ex-student, even if I was an academic basket case? The primary school even has a Dead Ringer Band room, which we're pretty chuffed about.

I did get nervous before going on stage back then, but it was a good feeling; expectation, I suppose. I loved it, both the singing and acting parts. I was a ham, without doubt. And of course I loved the fact that I got the lead roles. Drama was pretty much the only time I felt as though I really belonged at school.

I'd often wag school, come back in for drama, which I loved – not music, mind you, which I didn't take to at all, because I already had the best music teacher on the planet in Dad – and then disappear again. It'd be a risk coming back, for fear of being spotted by other teachers, but I loved drama so much that I couldn't resist. No wonder I got caught out sometimes.

One of my biggest disappointments from high school days was getting bumped from the lead role in a production because I'd lost my voice while singing with the Ringers. I guess that was bound to happen, given that the Dead Ringers were playing long gigs, in smoky bars, without any foldback, which meant I'd have to sing louder to be heard above the band and the noise. My parents took me to a specialist in Mount Gambier, an absolute fool, who recommended I not speak for six months. So there I was, 14 years old, communicating via notes I'd scribble on a note pad that I'd carry around with me. That lasted all of three weeks. Mum and Dad could see that it was impossible for me not to talk. But I did lose the lead role, and was given a non-speaking part, something that bugs me to this very day.

I've always been at ease with different sorts of people. At school I could hang out with the popular girls, and my closest friend, Ann Telfer, was academic – unlike me. I would spend a bit of time with my cousin Candy, who was a few years older and seemed a little wild, at least to me. It was Candy who asked me to come and smoke my first cigarette, and we headed off to some nearby scrub. But the matches weren't catching and she'd throw away every one that didn't light. Next thing we knew, the scrub all around us was burning. We tried patting it down and stomping on the flames, but nothing worked. 'Oh shit,' I asked her. 'What do we do?' We ran, of course. We told Mum that we'd seen a fire, but we certainly weren't going to admit that we started it. The local fire brigade had to come and put it out. We burned an entire area. It was years before either of us owned up to it, although everyone knew that Candy and I were responsible.

When not accidentally starting fires, I'd hang out with the Waggers, who I guess were the unpopular kids at school. There were some interesting people in the group, including a guy called Brendan Little, who, sadly, committed suicide not long after leaving school. He was a very mixed-up kid. Teachers didn't like him, either, and he copped the blame for anything that went wrong. An indigenous kid, Seth Dodd, was also part of the group. Then there was Leon Black, who later died in a car crash, and Damian Walker, the new kid in town. We'd all meet at a spot in the bush where we'd sit around a fire we built and talk; it was like our own little 'Breakfast Club', one of my favourite movies (curiously, there were also five mixed-up kids in the film). I was the only girl there, ever.

The Waggers accepted me but found it odd that I was there. 'You have a great family who care for you, what are you doing here?' they'd ask me. And I didn't have an answer for them, because I simply didn't know. My parents knew that I skipped school, and weren't happy that I did, but they also knew I was relatively safe. Notes would be sent home, and I'd talk my way out of trouble, using excuses like, 'I only missed roll call', or whatever. Mum probably didn't believe me, and she once actually came to the campfire – she'd been tipped off by Nash, a serial wagger himself, who knew all the spots – and dragged me back to school. But it was pretty clear that I was about to follow in the long line of Chambers' high school dropouts.

There were a couple of really low points; one where I took all these pills that I found in the glovebox of a friend's car. There were about ten in all. I can't recall what they were, most probably headache tablets. But as soon as I swallowed the pills, I let someone know what I'd done and they went and told my parents.

I know I didn't want to hurt myself, but I definitely didn't understand the seriousness of what I'd done. Maybe it was a stereotypical cry for help, although it could have been more a case of wanting everyone to know how messed up I was feeling, but not having the words to express it. Mum and Dad rushed me to the one doctor in town – there's no hospital nearby – and he gave me something to make me vomit, which I continued to do for the next few days. I'd never felt sicker; it was dreadful. I could barely move.

During this strange period I also tried to run away from home. I'd met this guy named Shannon Degarris who was from the bigger nearby township of Mount Gambier. He was tall, red-haired, freckled; he must have been in his late teens, quite a bit older than me. We weren't involved or anything; when I met Shannon he'd spent a bit of time living on the streets and I thought of him as another wayward lamb I felt I had to save.

On this particular day I got off the bus to my school, Millicent High, like normal, but left the schoolground and started walking out of town, towards Mount Gambier. Then I hitched a ride with a truckie. It didn't enter my mind that I could be in danger; I just spun a story for the truckie, saying I'd missed the school bus and was now running late.

Mount Gambier was the place where we went for a 'big shop', maybe once every couple of weeks, so I kind of knew the township. I spent the first half of the day wandering the town looking for Shannon. I had no firm plans apart from hanging out with him, convinced only he could know how I was feeling. Eventually I found him on the street when it was getting quite late and dark.

'Do your parents know you're here? What are you doing here?' he asked me, looking very surprised.

Shannon brought me to my senses a bit. He told me how fortunate I was, and that there was no sense in what I was doing.

'You shouldn't blow it at home, you know,' he said to me. 'Can you get back to Southend?'

In the end I went to the house of my Aunt Meredith, who lived in Mount Gambier and who I'd seen earlier that day – I'd lied, telling here I was in town with a friend. By this time my poor parents had called everyone, including Aunt Meredith, and were driving up to collect me. Strangely, I don't recall getting in trouble – which I feared – because Mum and Dad were so relieved that I was safe.

Though it must have been a nightmare time for them, they never made me feel that. Instead, they'd explain why I had to be punished for going off the rails, but they also pleaded with me to explain what I was feeling and going through. They did everything right. I really just had to grow out of it, and they had to find a way to hang in there until I did.

4

Metal and me

Beccy
Take my hand, my friend
This world's gone crazy.

Lyrics from 'Beccy'

Thankfully, there was one outlet for my teenage frustration – music. It was the only thing I could safely say I was any good at, the only thing which didn't make me feel all wrong. And it was the friends I made through music, especially Kym Warner and Beccy Cole, who lifted me out of this heavy state of mind I'd sunk into.

I was about 14 when I met Kym. It was on a night when I'd been planning to catch up with my Southend friends but Dad said no, I should stay home: 'My old mate Trev Warner, who I used to play with in bands before you were born, is coming from Adelaide to visit.'

He told me Trev had a son about my age, and I thought, 'Big deal.'

Dad also told me that the son, Kym, loved bluegrass and was a great mandolin player. Now, I had nothing against either, but I'd never met a teenager who was into bluegrass and in my adolescent, know-it-all way, I assumed he had to be a dag.

Mum and Dad were insistent on me staying and meeting the Warners. So when they arrived I was in a particularly shitty mood – which changed as soon as Kym walked in the door. Here was this very cool, handsome, Italian-looking guy, roughly my age, wearing an AC/DC T-shirt and carrying a mandolin. I was now very happy to be staying home, thank you.

As the night progressed, once we got over the uncomfortable part of getting to know each other with our parents looking on beaming, everyone went out to the veranda. Kym broke out his mandolin and we all started jamming. Aside from being so cute, and so funny, Kym was this incredible muso. What was not to like? I developed a crush on him straight out of the box – a bit of a habit of mine – that over time turned into a lifelong friendship. (Today he's part of a US-based trio called the Greencards, who have been nominated for two Grammys, and are very well known and respected in American bluegrass circles.)

One of the many interesting things about Kym was his broad musical taste. He loved country music but he loved a lot of other things too; heavy metal for instance. Partly because my parents hated it, partly because my giant crush on Kym meant I had to like what he liked, I became a huge metal fan for a time. Mötley Crüe and Metallica were my guys, and I fell pretty hard for Nikki Sixx from Mötley Crüe. I had more posters and photos of Nikki than anyone else: all over my schoolbooks, everywhere. When I noticed that Nikki wore this necklace with a skull ring and four little links, I searched everywhere to find the exact same one. I had a poster of Nikki Sixx next to a poster of Bela Fleck, one of the world's best banjo players. I didn't think it was weird; neither did Kym.

Soon after we met, Kym told me about an American band playing in Adelaide at the university. 'Do you want to come?' he asked. 'It'll cost $20 to get in.' I'd never heard of the band and told him that I really wanted to buy a tape with the only $20 that I did have. He said, 'Well, buy a tape of the band I'm about to see, because you'll be hearing about them soon enough. They're called Nirvana.' So I missed out on seeing them and bought their album *Nevermind* instead which I loved. Though I slavishly followed Kym's tastes for a while, there were a few bands that I simply liked because they sounded good. Nirvana was one of those.

Up till then I'd never felt a musical bond with anyone except my dad. Other friends were obsessed with music, but they were obsessed by what was on the Top 40 or what was cool. Kym knew about music – and though he was cool he didn't let that determine what he listened to. Just meeting someone like that was therapeutic for me and to top it off he was easy and fun to be with.

The Warners lived in Adelaide so Kym and I had a friendship through letters – we wrote loads of them to each other. When we visited their family, which we did every couple of months, he and I would sit and talk until the sun came up, while everyone else slept. Sometimes we'd talk about how we felt, sometimes it was about music, other times we'd just lie there and listen to records.

Kym has a great, slightly smartarse sense of humour, so we would indulge in all the normal teenage scoffing – how lame was this, how bad was that, while also celebrating all that was good in music (in our eyes). I did, however, keep quiet about the fact that I was still playing pop queen Laura Branigan at home.

Kym would play a bluegrass record and then Metallica; we'd be listening to these filthy guitar riffs while talking about the king of the mandolin, Bill Monroe. At the Warners' house, Kym, Dad and Trev and I would go into a room at the rear of their house and jam for hours on end. I looked forward to those visits enormously. And if Beccy Sturtzel was coming over, better still.

Meeting Bec – now better known as the singer Beccy Cole – was just as important for me as meting Kym, in a slightly different way. Bec was also a Seventh Day Adventist, and she seems to think that she was wearing her Adventist school uniform on the day we met at the Warners' house. Bec came from Adelaide – her mother, Carole Sturtzel, was well known within country music circles in South Australia, and Bec began singing with her mother's band when she was 14, in 1986. Her parents had split up when she was quite young, and the Warners treated Bec like one of their own, just as we did with Worm.

By the time Bec and I met we'd heard enough about each other from Kym to make us feel nervous, but we clicked right away. I knew that she was a huge Dolly Parton fan, long before it became hip to like Dolly. She also loved Tammy Wynette and Loretta Lynn, but she had modelled herself on Dolly Parton. On paper she even resembles her; blonde hair, big boobs and an outgoing, fearless personality. The first night we met she sang Tammy's 'Stand By Your Man' and her powerful voice left me thunderstruck – I had never hear a girl sing that way before. No way could I match her!

As is my way, I wanted to be like Bec as soon as I met her. She was so worldly – you know, she'd done gigs outside of Southend. And she was just a blast. We'd play around singing the Judds' songs together – the Judds, Naomi and Wynonna, a famous American mother/daughter act, were the biggest thing in country at the time. They are like walking country singer clichés with their big hair and tumultuous personal lives which lend credence to their songs of heartbreak. For a time, we actually wanted to become the Judds, minus all the drama and the hair – although maybe we did want the big hair, looking back at some old photos. We'd also sing Tanya Tucker's 'Strong Enough to Bend'.

Bec was the first girl I'd met who loved country music like I did. Till then I'd thought I was the only one in the world who knew this music; especially the more obscure names and songs. None of my friends from school were aware of it, when we talked about music it was about rock or metal or pop. Country music is so cordoned off from regular radio or television that you never have to hear it unless you seek it out – and most 14-year-old girls are not seeking it out. But when I met Bec she could match me song for song, artist for artist, not only on what was current, but on all the records Dad had introduced me to. When I met Bec she was singing Nanci Griffith, American country stuff that not many people were aware of.

Even though Bec was older than me, once I got to know her I started to see that she was a bit of a lost soul who needed a friend. She and I would sit up all night, often talking, sometimes crying, playing and talking music. We didn't talk about anything specific, just adolescent angst stuff, but it really helped me; it was comforting to know that someone I thought of as older and wiser could also feel so messed up.

Around then, another life-changing moment happened to me. Roseanne Cash, Johnny Cash's daughter, was touring Australia, and it went without saying that Dad and I would go and see her. Bec and Kym came along, as did Mum and Nash. I'd been to a few big shows – my first was Brian Cadd and Max Merritt in Mount Gambier. I'd also seen Melissa Etheridge, on her Brave & Crazy tour, when she played at the Thebarton Theatre in Adelaide and thought she was great. But this 1992 gig was different, in many ways.

I was a big fan of Roseanne Cash, but there were two other names on the bill I didn't know: Mary Chapin Carpenter and Lucinda Williams. It was a triple-header; they were all on stage together and would sing individually and then also sing with each other. It was an interesting, unusual format.

Lucinda Williams came out first, and I have to admit that initially she was my least favourite of the three. To give it some context, the singers I admired were graceful, angelic-sounding women like Emmylou Harris. If you've heard and seen Emmylou you'll know her pretty, pure voice and her elegant manner. Lucinda was nothing like that. She sounded almost like a blues singer, raw and rusty, and she looked like a grungy rock chick; maybe a bit like Chrissie Hynde. She was … cool. And country music is just not supposed to be cool.

And there were the songs: I'd never really heard a woman wear her heart so openly on her sleeve, or expose that much of her soul. Aside from Emmylou, most of my influences till that point were men: Hank Williams, Jimmie Rodgers, the Amazing Rhythm Aces, Larry Gatlin, plus the metal dudes I'd heard through Kym. And until that night spent watching Lucinda, I hadn't thought too hard about the notion of words, lyrics, gelling with music, even though I'm sure I knew about it subconsciously.

Lucinda was clearly singing her own songs about her own life. Her lyrics weren't cryptic, as so many lyrics can be: she said precisely, directly what she felt. And yet it was poetic and melodic and beautiful. As she launched into her first song, 'The Night's Too Long', my initial instinct was negative – what is this? – but by the end of the show I turned to Dad and said: 'I want to be her, I want to do what she's doing. I want to write songs and sing them.' I was a believer!

Everything about Lucinda Williams, from the way she presented her songs to the language she used, her melodies and her presence, completely enthralled me. I now saw music as the perfect way to express my feelings. I'd gotten a taste of a 'real' singer-songwriter, and I loved what I'd heard. That concert was absolutely massive for me, a huge moment in my creative life. And so my long-lasting relationship with Lucinda, who'd become a mentor and a friend, began in an unexpected way, as would so often be the case in my life.

As soon as I got home from the show I tried writing for the first time, and came up with a sort-of valentine to my new friend, a song I called 'Beccy'. It wasn't especially poetic, and it was quite the weepie, but I was proud of it. It was my way of saying, 'Hey, I know you're troubled.' I wanted to let Bec know that I was here for her, and the best way for me to do that was write a song. It was surprisingly easy. I sat down with a guitar, humming and playing, and came up with a song on my own. Songwriting was something I really took to.

It was a real moment for me. I was pretty nervous about playing it to Bec, so I first played it to Dad, something I continue to do to this day. But when I did play it to Bec she burst into tears and told me that it was the most beautiful thing she'd ever heard. It was a friend singing to a friend:

Beccy, take my hand, my friend
This world's gone crazy
But it's not the end.

Very genuine, totally earnest. She still says it's her favourite song. I believe her. Why shouldn't I?

Nash, Kym, Bec and I hung out together as much as possible. Nash and Bec were the same age, as were Kym and I, so it was a pretty natural fit. We started this jam band and learned songs that weren't coming from our parents – the first time in my life that I hadn't looked to Dad for musical guidance. We called ourselves the Brown Smelly Shits, which didn't really take off, strangely enough. But it was such a joy and a relief to feel this bond, and to have something to do which I didn't suck at.

Becoming close with these people, and hanging out more and more back in Beachport with Worm, who was fast becoming my best friend – Ernie to my Bert – really healed me. Music was now becoming more than just a part of my life; it was more like a way of life. It was something that I was getting excited about. I wanted to buy more records and I wanted Mötley Crüe posters all over my walls. I wanted to talk music and life with Kym and Bec until we'd cleared the room. I didn't care what anyone else thought. I felt liberated, free.

Another key player in our little troupe was a guy named Bryan De Gruchy. We called him 'Grumpy Old Gruch', although he was anything but that. He's another very funny, very dry guy, about my dad's age. And he's a luthier, a maker of stringed instruments, a very well respected craftsman and obviously a great guy to know. Dad asked him to custom-build a guitar for my 14th birthday, which was an amazing gift.

Whenever we would visit the Warner family, Gruch would come down from the Adelaide hills with all his new instruments, which were ours to try out. Alice, Gruch's wife, would come along as well, and all the women would hang out in the kitchen, while Mardi, Kym's mother, made great Italian food. Then we'd sit in the back room and jam old country and bluegrass songs. Everyone else would go to bed and Kym and I would lie awake, talking and listening to records. It was a magical time.

I hadn't given that much thought to my future; I had vague plans to become a nanny. I knew I wanted to have children, I knew I wanted to travel overseas, that was about the extent of my ambitions. But music was now becoming a whole way of life. I played with our jam band, and I played with the Dead Ringers. Kym and Bec and I would enter all the local talent quests at the Port Pirie Festival and elsewhere in South Australia, sometimes with the Dead Ringers, sometimes on our own. We'd enter every category we could; Kym went for Best Instrumental and Bec and I would go up against each other in Best Female and the band together for Best Duo. It was mostly fun, but you could win prize money and you might get an actual gig at the following year's festival which could get you a bit of exposure. It was also an eye-opener in terms of country music politics.

If you were going to sing country, you had to look country and we didn't look the part. It would have been the same if we'd shown up at, say, a rock music tryout, in big hats and cowboy boots instead of a leather jacket, jeans and deathlike gaze: they wouldn't have taken us seriously either. At the country music talent quests, our typical teenage grunge wear looked out of place among all the belt buckles and Western shirts. I remember hearing that we would have won one contest but Bec and I were wearing thongs, not boots – mainly because it was boiling hot. Even Mum and Dad, who didn't look grungy, didn't look country enough either in their normal jeans and shirts.

And we also didn't sing what passed for 'country music' in some circles. This is always a debating point – people spend hours talking about what is country and what isn't. But the definitions are often so narrow; to me, some of what Paul Kelly sings, or Bob Dylan or the Rolling Stones is as country-sounding as half the acts on the circuit. Country music has a certain sound and an emotional feel; it's hard to define but you know it when you hear it.

My own feeling is that like any art form country music is constantly changing and, while I love it, I want to push its boundaries. There's an argument that says, before doing that you need to understand its roots – well I agree. But I also felt that that I'd earned that right; I'd grown up with country, I had an instinct for it. It was part of who I was. But most people like putting music into clear categories and we didn't fit the common category of country music.

But so what? We were getting to play and the Dead Ringers were getting some gigs outside our town. In our heads we were already world famous – it couldn't get any bigger than this.

5

'It's Slim Dusty here'

Me, I'm from a small town
But I've been spending most of my time away
But I still hear you every time the wind blows
And it sounds just like yesterday.

Lyrics from 'Song For Gram'

Back in 1991, Uncle Kev Chambers had heard on the radio that Slim Dusty was on the lookout for songs that talked about the terrible drought then wreaking havoc on Australian farms – and on farmers. When he found out, Dad decided that he was just the man to write the song. He came up with a tune called 'Things Are Not the Same on the Land', got it down on cassette, and sent it off to Slim's people. It was all a bit of wishful thinking on his part – really, what chance was there that this Oz icon would record the song of an ex-fox hunter who hadn't written anything until he was 40? Yet about a month later, at seven in the morning, our phone rang.

'Hello,' said the vaguely familiar, slightly crusty voice down the line. 'It's Slim Dusty here.'

Dad wasn't convinced. 'Oh, bullshit,' he snapped back, but even though he was about to hang up, he decided against it, just in case. And it really was Slim, who told Dad that he loved the song and was just about to record it. Dad couldn't believe his luck. A little while later, Dad received a personal note of thanks in the mail from Slim along with a tape recording of the song, preceded by a little introduction.

'Hey, Bill,' the great man said, 'we're now in the studio recording your song. Hope you like it.'

If the entire thing had ended there, Dad would have been the happiest man in Southend, maybe even all of Australia. Slim Dusty, who he'd admired forever, liked his song enough to record it: where could he go from here?

But then came another unexpected phone call. It was Terry Hill from BAL Marketing telling Dad that 'Things Are Not the Same on the Land' had been nominated for a Golden Guitar, in the upcoming awards, to be held in Tamworth in January 1992. We were all so thrilled, completely over the moon, even if Dad had to ask: 'What's a Golden Guitar?'

Basically, when it came to the business of music, we were hillbillies. It hadn't touched us yet. We had no need of agents, promoters, 'door deals' – or awards. Mum booked our gigs by ringing pubs and asking if they needed a band. If the publican needed to hear us beforehand we had a couple of homemade tape recordings. We had one titled *Kindred Spirits* that we sold at gigs – so we didn't need a record label either! And that was about it.

We had vaguely heard of the Grammys, the biggest music awards in the world, and Mum and Dad probably knew that Tamworth had a Country Music Festival but it wasn't really on our radar all the way up there in NSW.

Still, the BAL rep told Dad enough to convince him that come January we should pack up the car and head north to Tamworth. As we had had to close the fish shop – it had become too difficult to do both music and run a business – Dad was working at the local fish-processing factory, with the result that we couldn't afford the fuel or accommodation. But with the financial help of family and friends we were able to get to Tamworth.

We figured it would be a breeze: we'd simply set up a swag outside of town, then roll up to the bar of a few local pubs and ask the publican if we could play. Bec, Trev and Kym were playing in the band then, and Worm also came along for the trip (and the cold beer). It was only Tamworth, we figured, how tricky could it be to get a gig?

Very tricky, as we soon found out. For most of the year Tamworth is a normal rural township, but for the two weeks that the festival is on, it attracts thousands of country-music lovers from around the nation and industry people from every known label. When we knocked on doors, publicans and bookers informed us that most festival gigs are set up months, even years, in advance. 'The Dead who band?' they asked, before guiding us back out onto Peel Street, the town's main drag, where we fell into step with the other tourists.

In one sense, it was the right time to be at the festival. The Australian country music industry was going through a bit of a boom off the breakout success of James Blundell. James was young and good-looking, he played country rock, which was replacing the older style of music Slim Dusty sang, he was even getting mainstream radio airplay for his hit song 'Way Out West'. He had made country commercial again, so A & R guys from big labels were all in Tamworth looking to find the next James Blundell.

A year or so later Lee Kernaghan would take over James's patch with an even more massive album and hit song, *Boys from the Bush*, though Lee was strictly a country act, not a crossover. So what had been a sleepy country music festival, all cowshit and sheds, was at the start of a professional transformation in the early 1990s.

For us, that meant that there was no chance we could get a gig. Finally though, after wandering around Tamworth for a while, we had a small victory. The publican at the Central Hotel, one of the many Peel Street venues, told us it was okay if we busked outside his pub.

Our setup looked a bit odd: Bec and me, two young girls, out front singing; a woman, Mum, on bass; Nash playing drums while standing up; Kym and Trev on mandolin and fiddle; and my dad picking some fancy guitar. But the crowd seemed to like what they heard, because in a short time our initially curious gathering had swelled to about 500 people. We took the hat around that night, too, and collected about $500, a fortune for us.

The good thing about places like Tamworth is that a busking

act can command attention, because that's why people are there, to hear music. When we returned to the same spot the next night, a bigger crowd, something like 800 punters, showed up, as word got around town about this family band. We played there every night for the week we were there. We'd never made so much money from music in our lives, or been so well received. We'd never really even played to a crowd before.

The Golden Guitar awards were held over a few days in a big shed. There was no red carpet or anything back then; I don't think we even had seats, we just stood around on the dirt floor, but we were so excited to be there we didn't mind. Dad had no acceptance speech as he didn't expect to win Song of the Year so when he did he was almost speechless – which for him is really something. Ted Egan, another country singing legend, presented him with his award and then he went off to do two hours of radio interviews. It capped off an unforgettable week for all of us.

Tamworth was a turning point; it was the first time we started thinking maybe we could make a living from music. The applause had definitely got to us! A rep who had seen us busking had booked the band to appear at the next Gympie Muster, a big Queensland country music event which attracted crowds of 20,000 or more. A guy called Keith Melbourne, who managed acts like Ray Kernaghan, Lee's dad, and Buddy Williams, offered to manage us and help us find gigs. People who we didn't even know had liked what we played! Suddenly we had a glimpse of a world beyond Southend – if not much idea of how to reach it.

As we neared the end of our lengthy drive home from Tamworth, we reached the turn off into Southend. As Dad drove on, we all noticed something strange: on every second roadside post there would be a poster congratulating 'Bill Chambers and the Dead Ringer Band'. The whole town had pitched in and made these dedications to our unexpected win. When we got to our house, the locals had decked it out in streamers and balloons, while someone had baked a massive guitar-shaped cake. It was such a wonderful community gesture – we were as thrilled by Southend's response as the town was by our win.

As the night wore on, Kym and Bec stepped forward and announced that they had their own little tribute, a song of their own, for all of us. They cleared their throats, smiled and began to strum a tune that was strangely similar to Dad's 'Things Are Not the Same on the Land'. One big difference – their version was titled 'Things Are Not the Same Down my Pants'. It was one of the funniest songs I'd ever heard, even funnier than 'Kasey', and it just showed why these were two of my favourite people: they could be so hilarious and so, so clever. Dad was doubled up in laughter. He said that hearing the song was even better than winning the Golden Guitar.

Life was changing, not just for me, but for all of us. The Dead Ringer Band was about to hit the highway, and our lives were set to take a different path than we could ever have predicted. It was almost as if we'd returned to the Nullarbor, but instead of hunting foxes we were now belting out country songs.

6

'This woman just said that they want to, erm, spend the night with all of us'

Tonight I must be gypsy bound
You'll never know where I'll be hanging 'round.

Lyrics from 'Gypsy Bound'

In the wake of Dad's surprise win at Tamworth, the Dead Ringer Band started to develop what would best be described as a 'little buzz'. It wasn't as though the music world was beating a path to our front door, but the work became pretty steady. The four of us, Nash, me, Mum and Dad – were playing everywhere from Townsville in the north to Coober Pedy in the south and Broome and Esperance in the west, covering around 50,000 kilometres a year in our trusty Landcruiser with the trailer full of instruments in tow, often sleeping in swags by the side of the highway. Between 1993 and 1994 we played over 130 shows. It was the Nullarbor all over again, but with a musical twist.

There were some advantages in being a family band – as

opposed to a solo act – and one of them was being able to tour like this. For a solo act, it would have been close to impossible – there wasn't much money in it and a solo singer would have had to pay for a band, fuel and accommodation. We came with a built-in band, we could all travel in the same car – along with Worm who was like a third child by then, and a sort of roadie – and as for accommodation, we were used to sleeping rough. We slept on the road in the rain, once in the snow. If we didn't have money for food, we would do some hunting and make kangaroo tail soup or a rabbit stew or we caught some fish. It was very much the way Slim Dusty had done it; touring all over the country with his family – so there was a precedent.

Keith Melbourne – whom we had met at Tamworth – worked hard at getting us gigs and at filling us in with how the business worked. Keith was 'old school' so I'm not sure what he made of us but he definitely seemed to have our interests at heart. We also had Mum who was still booking us into gigs too. She would ring up outback pubs with her pitch: 'We're a country band from South Australia and we charge $400 for a gig.' Straightforward. It was all about word of mouth: one publican would tell another about us and the word would spread. Sometimes we'd go out for three months, really tour hard and we didn't need to supplement our income with hunting.

For Nash and me, this was a great time. Nash had dropped out of school as soon as he was able, and by the time I was 15, I was more or less not going to school. I was doing a childcare course by correspondence, studying in the back of the car as we travelled, but

I was otherwise free. So our job was to play in a band and travel around the country. Nash, who was by then around 18, reaped the benefits of being young, good-looking – and a musician. Now and again we'd notice that the same girls would turn up to gigs; sometimes we'd collect him the next morning from some fan's house. My parents didn't cramp his style – they were very relaxed with things like that.

There were some drawbacks to our life on the road of course. Once we were on the highway, somewhere near Wagga in NSW, when we had an engine fire; smoke and flames started belching out from under the hood of the car. We pulled over and hurriedly unhitched the trailer as the fire got bigger; if nothing else, we needed to save our instruments. Then we warily approached the car and grabbed what clothes and other essentials we could get our hands on. So there we were, standing beside our blazing car, stranded on the highway, waiting for help, when Mum remembered that she'd stashed all our money, about $1000, in a safe spot under the dash. It went up in smoke, along with the car.

I also had my worst experience with sleep disorders while we were on tour. I was 16 at the time, really sick, feverish – and a fever, as I've learned, can bring it on. We were in Gundagai, NSW, playing in the packed back room of this club. We would play all night, broken into four, one-hour-long sets with short 'breathers' in between. I was in really bad shape, so much so that I kept leaving the stage during the first set to vomit. Lying on the backstage floor I had just enough strength to lift my head and throw up.

At the end of the first set Mum decided I was too sick to continue. We were staying about a block away from the gig, so during the break Mum walked me back to the cheap motel where we staying that night and put me to bed.

I was so wrecked I went straight to sleep and Mum left to continue the gig. But somewhere during the night I got up, although still asleep, opened the door and got outside the motel room. I remember some of the events of that night, but not waking up and leaving our room. It had to be around midnight – our gigs usually started at 8 or 9 pm and went on for at least four hours.

It was a terrible attack; I can remember clearly wandering around the carpark of the motel in the undies and T-shirt I'd worn to bed, hysterical, sobbing wildly and feeling terrified of something – I don't know what. Then I walked down the block and crossed the road to where the gig was, still fast asleep and still crying. Thank God it wasn't a highway. I made it to the venue safely, but when I got there the back door was locked and I could hear the band playing inside. I stood outside for a while – I have no idea how long – sobbing, banging on this door, crying out for help, but no one heard me so eventually I gave up and sat down on a nearby step, my head in my hands, sobbing quietly. Then a couple of drunks fell out the back door, hardly noticing me sitting there. They walked out leaving the door open. I quickly jumped up and grabbed the door – still sleepwalking – and went inside, in my 'evening wear'.

There was a little hallway at the back of the room, opposite where the band was playing, which is where I ended up, behind the crowd. I looked up and saw my mum on stage, and she saw me. Straight away, she knew that I was sleepwalking; she could see it in my eyes, in my face. And as soon as I looked at her, I woke up. Bang! It wasn't like in the movies, all that, 'Oh, where am I?' crap. I knew that I'd walked there and that I'd been asleep.

It's funny looking back on it, but it definitely wasn't funny at the time. A teenage girl, sleepwalking around a country town late at night in her undies and T-shirt; anything could have happened. It left my mum really shaken, partly because I think she thought I was getting over it by then. Seeing the ragged emotional state I was in she left Nash and Dad to bump out the gear, took me back to the hotel and put me to bed.

Being on the road means spending a lot of time in the car, looking for ways to fill the hours. We'd work on our songs – some, like 'Halfway to Sydney', were written in the car (it was actually called 'Indian Pacific' until we found out that Slim Dusty had a song by the same name).

For my 16th birthday, after much badgering on my part, my parents bought me a banjo. There weren't that many female banjo players, so I thought it might be a nice little niche. Playing the banjo is actually pretty hard, and a poorly played banjo is second only to a badly played fiddle in terms of sounds to be avoided – so everyone insisted that I go off into the bush to practise.

To help me out, Dad designed a practice banjo, a round piece of wood with a little neck attached. And it had five strings, just like a regular banjo, but he padded it down so you couldn't hear anything which meant I could practise in the car. A big part of banjo playing is mastering what are called 'rolls', which is like fingerpicking on an acoustic guitar. I spent many long hours sitting in the back of the Landcruiser, silently plucking my practice banjo, until eventually I realised I was never going to be a natural player.

Sometimes there were little interviews to do which we'd set up with community radio stations, basically to plug our upcoming shows. These sitdowns didn't always go according to plan. During an interview with a DJ in Albury we decided to give away a Dead Ringers album to the first caller. 'Right, we'll go to the phones now,' said the DJ – and not a single person phoned in. Not one. We all sat there feeling stupid, waiting for the phone to ring. In the end we pretended someone had called and staged a fake conversation with the 'winner'.

At another community station, in outback Victoria, the DJ mixed up the buttons on his desk, which meant that everything we said during the interview didn't go to air. While we thought we were off air we grumbled about the gig we'd played the night before, where no one had turned up – and that's what the listeners heard. Not so good.

Sometimes we had other people come along, which made a change from talking to each other. Bec was a Dead Ringer for about six months, but both she and Kym moved on to their own careers, although we all stayed close friends. Other times we'd take BJ Barker, a heavy-metal guy from Mount Gambier who we met and countryfied, out with us to play on drums. BJ was great for us because he needed saving and rescuing so both Mum and I could work overtime on that. His parents had died when he was a teenager and he pretty much raised himself, sometimes on the streets, doing it rough.

We took along people whose company we enjoyed and who could deal with our lives – you really need to get on when you spend so much time together. Pete Drummond, whose father is Pat Drummond, a country-folk muso, would sometimes play with us and neither he nor BJ minded if there wasn't much money or if they had to sleep on a patch of dirt. And of course there was always Worm, who would be lugging gear, working the lights and helping out wherever he could. Frankly, I would have had him along even if he didn't do a thing, because he was my mate, but in any case he wasn't the kind of guy who'd sit around while everyone else was busy.

I don't know why I felt so comfortable with Worm; I just did. Though we didn't have that musical bond that I had with Kym, I also didn't have to worry about being cool enough – like I did with Kym. Everyone needs someone in their lives with whom they can be their 100% daggy self and for Worm and me, we were each other's someone. I never felt judged by him, no matter what.

That was important because by this stage we were starting to get the sense of how much we were outsiders in the music business. In the country music business in particular. It really hit home when we were asked to be a part of a country music tour. It was the promise of steady work and we couldn't afford to turn it down – and it was also a glimpse into a whole other world.

As we were the least known act on the tour, our job was to open the show. There were a number of other guest acts, leading up to the star, so it was all a bit like Monty Python's Flying Circus with everyone doing different things. There was even an Elvis impersonator. It wasn't until the tour started that it hit us that we really didn't belong there. The main act was very much a cabaret country star; he would sweep out on stage all in black, talk to the ladies, throw them flowers and sing. Which was fine except that our act, as far as we had one, was the polar opposite; we came out, Nash and me in our jeans and messy long hair, both of us wearing eyeliner and by then sporting a few piercings – played our eight songs, mumbled a few words and left.

We weren't actually that out there – at an event like Homebake or Big Day Out we would have looked pretty normal. But in that arena we came across like Kurt Cobain opening for Wayne Newton. Nobody seemed to care about what we were playing or singing; the focus was on other things. My swearing seemed to make people on the tour cringe. Nash got yelled at once for wearing a black shirt on stage because, 'Only the star of the show wears a black shirt'. Another day when his shoes had fallen apart, he borrowed a pair of cowboy boots and got a thumbs up – I think that's the last time he wore cowboy boots.

It might have been okay if the tour had gone well, but it was going pretty badly. The main act had a following from years past;

As a kid, I was always laughing, smiling, singing,
constantly on the lookout for new experiences
and adventures.

That green jacket was one of
my favourite things to wear.
Fashion victim, me? Nah.

We divided our time between Southend in South Australia, where I was born, and the Nullarbor, where my dad worked. I couldn't imagine a better upbringing.

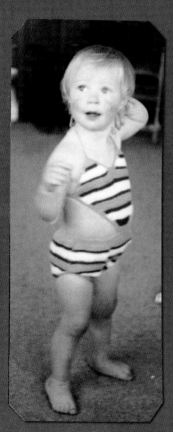

My mother, Diane Chambers.
When I had my own kids,
I asked her: 'How did you take
me out on the Nullarbor when
I was three weeks old *and not
lose your mind?*'

My dad, Bill Chambers.
I once wrote in some liner
notes: 'To my dad, who
taught me everything I know
about music.' It's true, too.

With my brother, Nash, who's always been there
for me, throughout my life. Oh, and that's our
intrepid poodle, Licky.

This photo of me and my dad was actually used for a campaign to promote Southend. And who says I was a tomboy?

Even when we were out on the Nullarbor, Mum would make Nash and me cakes for our birthdays. She bought the ingredients from the 'Tea and Sugar' train, which we caught up with every two weeks. That's me above in 1979, turning three, and below in 1983 on my seventh birthday.

Keeping clean was a huge challenge on the Nullarbor. We'd sometimes bathe at artesian bores, as Dad is doing here.

Did I mention that Nash has always been there to help me? He might have regretted it here; that's an outback toilet I'm sitting on.

That's Nash and me with Dad, dining out under the stars.
I was 12 months old at the time.

Even though it now seems very un-PC, we never thought twice about Dad's occupation. He was a fox hunter. And a pretty good one, too.

It wasn't quite a five-star life on the Nullarbor, as this shot of Nash and me at one of our camps proves. Still, we loved the life.

The highlight of almost every new stop on the Nullarbor was building our 'cubby'; that's Nash inside one of our grand designs.

Another Nullarbor birthday, April 1985. That's Nash and me with our cousins Clint, Narelle and Traci (from left), who sometimes travelled with us.

We kept all kinds of strange pets, even a kangaroo. Here I am with Jackson, a pet rabbit (named for Jackson Browne, of course).

I have such powerful memories
of growing up on the Nullarbor.
I sometimes think of myself as
an ambassador for the place!

Dear Nanna and Pa, Thank you for my presents I have new black boots to go with my dress.
Love from Kasey

One of my letters home from the Nullarbor.

My many faces and looks – and all this without a stylist!
Can you believe it?

With my friend Caddie Ellis. Caddie was with me when I first sang in public, aged nine. My eyes were shut the entire time.

unfortunately they were now quite elderly. A tour is an expensive thing and there would have been a lot of pressure to make back the money which had been invested in this one. Someone had to cop the blame; in the end it was us.

Halfway through the tour we were told that we were 'scaring people off' and so we were taken off the posters and TV ads. Then our songs were cut from eight to two. The way we saw it, we still got paid, and it had all become so painful by then that it was a relief to be more or less axed. It's true we weren't helping pull in the crowds since no one had heard of us; on the other hand ... I don't think that we were the problem!

The tour has become a sort of campfire story within our family – we laugh about the mismatch until we cry. In one way it was a great lesson – this was what we didn't want to be and it really taught us to say No to anything that felt wrong for us. At the risk of sounding a bit Oprah about it, it also confirmed for me that the right motivation is everything – I wanted to play music because it was a great way to connect with people. I didn't want to be driven by blind ambition or the wrong sort of ego. The funniest thing is that at the end of the tour the headliner pulled us aside and informed us all, 'You'll never work in this industry again.'

But before anyone starts feeling sorry for the lonely outcasts we'd become, let me say that, the tour aside, we had a lot of support as the Dead Ringers. We were getting airplay on John Nutting's show on the ABC, and from 2TM's Nick Erby among others.

And we had Slim Dusty and his wife, Joy McKean, flying the flag for us – as big a boost as you could get in country circles.

My first meeting with Slim was pretty funny, and further proof – if any more was needed – of just how green I truly was. Slim had invited Dad to 301 Studios in Sydney, to add some guitar to a track he was recording. This was a big moment, so the entire family came along. When we rang the studio buzzer, the man himself opened the door. But Slim wasn't wearing his trademark slouch hat, and I didn't recognise him at first – none of us did. I actually thought he was the doorman until we stepped inside and he introduced himself. I'm glad I didn't ask him where we could find Mr Dusty!

Slim would often check in with Dad to see if he had any new songs, which was incredibly flattering. I think because they'd done things a bit differently when they were starting out, Joy and Slim felt some affinity with us – and also they were just good cheerleaders for new acts, of all types. Like us, Slim and Joy enjoyed music, whether it came from Australia or America, whether it was 'pure' or a blend of other styles. If a few more alternative acts came up the country music ladder, well, they welcomed that. Slim presented me with my first award at Tamworth for *The Captain* some years later and I'm so grateful that he chose to do it by saying, 'Don't let anyone tell you this girl isn't country.' Who's going to argue with Slim?

By the time we returned to Tamworth in January 1993, we were headlining our own shows. We were now playing the leagues club, the RSL and The Longyard, 'proper' venues. It was the first time we'd taken the plunge and did a paying show. I think we played two in all. It was a really big room for us and we were stoked. But the night before the gig I caught a terrible flu; I was vomiting violently and was not in any shape to sing. But I was just so determined to do the gig. It was more than not wanting to let down the fans – I really wanted to do the show because I simply didn't want to miss out. I was a teenager; I was excited. We even rehearsed for it, which was a first.

The good thing about the Dead Ringers was that I had vocal back-ups in Dad and Nash, so if necessary they could do a gig without me. With that in mind we agreed that I'd rest up, and see if my health improved, although it was likely that I might have to miss the show. A Tamworth friend of ours, Andrew Claremont, a fiddle and mandolin player, had played with us once in Mount Gambier when Dad was sick. Andrew did some reiki on him, which seemed to magically cure his ailment. Dad mentioned this to me and I was up for anything that might help me get on stage.

'Sure, why not?' I groaned.

Andrew was in town but he had a gig and couldn't come over, but said that a friend of his – an unusual hippy woman – could do it, and he sent her around. (Andrew, a sometimes Dead Ringer, was a bit of a hippy himself: he once got us to pull over on the side of the highway and showed us how to cook a beetroot on the car's manifold. And we thought we knew how to improvise!)

Mum, Dad and Nash had already left for the sound check when this woman arrived. I was lying in bed, back at the motel, still really sick. I was drifting in and out of sleep the whole time, while she was doing whatever it was that she did. To be honest, I thought it was a crock of shit, but felt it was worth a try.

She started saying things to me, in this soft voice: 'You're on stage, you're fine, your toxins are gone, you'll sing like an angel', blah blah blah.

I just wanted her to leave me alone to vomit and cry, which eventually she did. Mum and Dad came back and I suggested that I shower and come down and sit backstage. Maybe I could come out later on in the gig, at least for one song. We agreed that was a good idea. I still felt dreadful.

They poured me into the car and we arrived backstage. John Nutting was the MC, and he was introducing the band while I was vomiting into a bin backstage. It was a bit rock and roll really, but without the booze or drugs. John knew I was sick, but didn't want to make a big deal of it. Mum and Dad would explain my situation to the crowd. But when they walked out I was right there with them. Mum glared at me, as if to say: 'What are you doing?'

Yet I proceeded to sing every song of the set, and think I sounded fine. I didn't mention that I was sick, and no one would have known. We played for 90 minutes and then I walked off stage and started throwing up all over again, even more violently than before. I was so sick they had to carry me to the car. I don't really buy into the 'world of the unexplained' too much; I laugh at it a bit. I don't totally disregard it, but you know, I'm pretty busy with the real world. Still, this was weird.

As the Dead Ringers' accidental career developed, we started thinking about moving from our home base in Southend. It wasn't that convenient when we were spending more and more time on the east coast. Nash, whose interests had always been broader than music, was starting to develop a management and business brain and the business was very much in NSW.

In 1994, on another road trip, we were driving through the NSW Central Coast when, through the car window, we saw a poster for Keith Urban, who was playing at the Avoca Beach Hotel.

'Well, that's it,' we decided in typical Team Chambers fashion. 'If a pub on the Central Coast is willing to book an unknown country act like Keith' – and Keith was still under the radar back then – 'then maybe it's the place for us. This could be a cool little town.'

Nash summed it up pretty well when he said: 'Yeah, this place is happening. It's got a beach, surf, you can fish here and Keith Urban plays at the pub.' It was decided, then and there, that we'd move, although we hung onto our house in Southend for some time afterwards.

Obviously leaving home wasn't a decision we made lightly. Although the Central Coast is in some ways very like Southend, with its fishing village feel, it was 2000 km from the rest of Dad's family, none of whom had moved more than a town or so away. While we had totally shed our religion by then, they were still Seventh Day Adventists with a wariness of cities. The idea of us moving to somewhere so far and so sinful – close to Sydney! – was alarming. They'd never have stood in the way, but Dad's nanna would still ring him to ask if he was safe and getting enough sleep. She did that for years after we kids were born.

Mum's family were a little more accepting – after all, she'd moved to Southend already and then to the Nullarbor, so the Central Coast wasn't such a shock. But for us the decision just made sense even if we had to live in a caravan park, as we did at first. It saved us time and money. Being based in Southend meant we would often travel for a week before getting to our first gig.

It wasn't long before Worm joined us on the coast, after an awful accident back home. He had been fishing back in Beachport, with one of his best mates, Brad. The sea was rough but Brad had gone in for a swim, and horribly, he got sucked under and drowned. Worm, who dived in to save him, had almost drowned as well. It took a few days for the authorities to find Brad's body.

When we heard about it we were on our way to Avoca from Southend but we turned around and came back to be with Worm.

It was a really hard time for him, dealing with the loss of his friend, and the inevitable guilt – though he couldn't have acted more courageously than he did – and he started drinking way too much, wallowing in alcohol. I could see that he was going to go off the rails, so we took him back with us to Avoca. Worm needed a new start in a new place; his parents were fine with him going; and he was so much a part of our group it felt like a natural thing to do.

When we eventually got a house, we borrowed some money from Dad's sister and brother-in-law to set up our own studio. It was a sort of sort musical laboratory for Nash, whose interest in the recording side of things had increased, too, as his enthusiasm for playing live started to decline. Jeff McCormack, a musician who lived nearby, would drop by and give Nash some tips about what plugged in where, and what happened when you pressed a certain button on the desk. Basic stuff. Step by step we were all finding our places in the music world – Dad's and mine were in writing and playing, Mum's and Nash's were the bigger picture. And we began finding niches for the kind of band we were.

An album we'd recorded titled *Red Desert Sky* made its way to Warren Fahey who ran Larrikin Records, the label of choice for such acts as Redgum, Kev Carmody and Eric Bogle. Fahey described it as 'a small label for interesting [Australian] music', and that suited us. Up until then, we'd been selling the tape of *Red Desert Sky* at gigs – we'd sold about 500 copies – but Larrikin licensed the record, added a new cover and re-released it on CD and tape in late 1993. It didn't sell millions, or even thousands, but it was one of the many stepping stones that kept popping up in front of us, helping us to become full-time musicians. Laurie Dunn and Kay Crick at Massive Records were also incredibly helpful and supportive. This would be the next label that the Dead Ringers would sign with.

There was one particular occasion on the road when I was really glad that Nash took charge. We'd met a line-dancing couple while in Tamworth, who'd come to most of our shows when we were in town. They were lovely people, but super-straight, or so I thought. They invited BJ, Nash and me out to their house for drinks after a gig. We soon found ourselves in the middle of a strip poker game, which BJ was losing, badly – he was down to his undies. I thought it was funny, mainly because I wasn't losing, and because BJ hadn't worn his best undies. Nash suddenly pulled me aside and said that we should go.

'Why?' I asked. 'I'm having fun.'

'Well,' he replied, 'this woman just said that they want to, erm, spend the night with all of us.'

'Nash, did you tell them that we're brother and sister?'

'Yep,' he said, 'and they don't seem to care.'

BJ collected his clothes and we bolted, laughing all the way back to town. Line dancers, of all people!

7

'Were you the girl with the big silver shoes?'

These pines are not the ones I'm used to
They won't carry me home when I cry
Am I too far gone to recover
Or can I turn if I try?

Lyrics from 'These Pines'

In May 1995, the Dead Ringers were invited to play at the annual country music festival on Norfolk Island, a drop in the South Pacific Ocean between Australia and New Zealand. It came on the heels of a second Golden Guitar for Group of the Year and the bit of attention we were getting from outside country circles meant we were getting more festival gigs – even a few at Tamworth.

I knew absolutely nothing about Norfolk. But from the moment we stepped off the plane I felt at home there. Apart from my time on the Nullarbor, I've spent much of my life surrounded by the ocean – fishing, the beach, those types of landmarks – and that was Norfolk all over.

The festival itself was an interesting experience. The Dead Ringers had been hired to play our own set, but as usual we were also required to back up the competitors in a talent competition. The organisers would pick a few artists from both New Zealand and Australia, who competed for the Trans Tasman Entertainer of the Year award. The Oz contender that year was Darren Coggan, a country boy from Wagga, who we gelled with from the get-go; he was a terrific hang, a lovely bloke, easy-going and friendly. And unlike most of the other competitors, 'Daz' wrote and sang his own songs. He was so great, so natural, both as a person and a performer, and I connected with him in the same way I'd connected with Bec and Kym. We all did.

As I watched Darren perform, as much as I liked his style I also feared that his originality might be his undoing: these sorts of events are normally won by the crowd-pleasers, the acts that play the favourites and pander to the audience. So you can imagine how impressed we were that the judges saw the same qualities in Darren that we did, and named him the winner. He was the underdog who'd come through and won, which reminded me of Dad's win at Tamworth a couple of years earlier. Darren was blown away; we all were. (Darren would become a Dead Ringer for a time, too.)

As the festival was winding down, two kids, whose names were Kurt and Gemma Menghetti, introduced themselves and invited us to their house for dinner. That's how things went socially on Norfolk; people were so open and friendly. We agreed straight away, and over dinner we got to meet all the family: two other children, and their Dad.

The Menghetti kids, who came from a mix of Polynesian and New Zealander backgrounds, were all beautiful, striking-looking, with distinctly different natures. Kurt was the oldest, and possibly the shyest person I've ever met, which might have been part of his appeal to me because I am the opposite. Dana was supermodel beautiful, tall and thin, even at 12. Gemma, the next one along, reminded me of the actress Karen Allen, who was in the film *Sweet Talker* that had been shot in Beachport; she was bubbly, full of spirit, a real people person, like me, and we got along well. Jess, who everyone called 'Wolfla' was the youngest, and he was quiet too, like his older brother.

Their mother, Sue, had passed away about six months earlier, and they'd been doing it hard, living with their dad (nicknamed 'Jap') in a farmhouse outside the town. But they had a lovely warmth and closeness which I found very attractive. In fact everything got a bit jumbled in my head – the beauty of the island, the welcoming nature of the Menghettis; I fell for the package. Eventually, I'd also fall for Kurt.

From then on I was a regular visitor to Norfolk. Something just drew me to the place, it's crept into several of my best-known songs and for a while I even lived there. Dad and Nash rarely came to Norfolk after that first trip, but Mum, Worm and I would visit for a week, then for two weeks, then a month, then three, then we moved in with Jap and the kids. I guess to an outsider it must have seemed pretty weird, but to me our crowded house felt perfectly natural. The kids took to Mum – because people always take to Mum – and we all fitted together. We'd only return to the mainland for tours. The rest of the time I made extra cash through a little cleaning business Kurt and I set up together on the Central Coast.

Kurt was a few years younger than me but even in the early part of our relationship when we were just friends, we became virtually inseparable, zipping around on his motorbike. In a really sweet gesture, Kurt and Dana gave me a love heart pendant that belonged to their mother, which I wore on my belly button for years. So it was no surprise to anyone – except me, who is always the last to see the obvious – when Kurt's and my friendship spilled over into a romance. I'd had a few boyfriends by this stage, but this was the first one which felt serious – for both of us.

I did write a song for Kurt: 'The Captain'. That was his nickname, and it arose out of a time when he called me on the phone once. I was back in Beachport and Worm's dad, 'Plummy', answered the phone.

'Who is it?' he asked.

'Kurt Menghetti', Kurt replied, but said it very quickly.

Plummy said to me: 'Captain Eddy is on the phone for you.'

The nickname stayed, or at least the Captain bit did.

People read all sorts of things into songs – we all do it – but that song has had some really strange interpretations; one woman asked me if it was about domestic violence! I think it's because the line 'You're the Captain, I am no one' makes it sound as if I feel overshadowed. The reality is that in Kurt's and my relationship I was the one who took the lead; I talked more, was more social, I even spent more time with his friends than he did. The song was a way of saying 'Let's trade roles, I want you to shine while I hang back'. Something which a loudmouth like me could never do, by the way.

When romance reared its head I took Kurt to Southend, to meet the rest of my Chambers family. He was the friend I mentioned at the start of the book who walked into Nanna's house and found the dead kangaroo hanging from a hook in the kitchen, a newspaper on the floor soaking up its blood. Two rabbits were in the sink waiting to be prepared.

Kurt is always quiet so he couldn't have got any quieter, but I could tell that he thought this was, well, a little bit unusual. For me it was a real reminder how far my life had travelled away from my roots.

That's okay. I'm proud of where I come from – and kangaroo remains one of my favourite meats. I eat it once a week, even now, although today I buy it from the supermarket, rather than having to hunt it, or prepare it in my front room.

After my first epiphany at the Lucinda Williams concert back in 1992, I'd seen Lucinda perform again. In fact I'd become a rabid fan, and we even had a link. I'd been to see her play her Sweet Old World Tour – driving five hours up to Adelaide from Beachport to be part of the reverential crowd in a large pub. The whole family were introduced to her backstage as 'local singers' and she signed our CDs for us. And later, through an American contact called John Lomax III, who'd taken an interest in the Ringers when we started getting regular gigs, she received some copies of our CDs.

One thing led to another, with the result that in 1996, the Dead Ringers, and Worm, went to America for the first time. It was a little bit because Lucinda started talking about us to various people but mainly because John Lomax worked hard to make it happen. John's own reputation helped; not only did he come from a famous musical family – his grandfather, John Avery Lomax, was a pioneering musicologist, who'd travel throughout the country's backwaters in the 1930s, recording obscure musical acts – but he had managed highly regarded singer-songwriters like Steve Earle and Townes Van Zandt.

I liked John, we all did; he was a warm, friendly guy, very far from a record executive shark – and we trusted that he was looking after our interests. The idea was that we would go to the US, play a few showcases, do some 'meet and greets' and try and stir up some record label interest.

In the end, not many people turned up to meet and greet us and the mythical recording deal fell apart, but that didn't make this trip any less memorable. It was our first trip overseas – and we were going to Nashville. Home to Johnny Cash and Emmylou Harris! In America. The place where people gave tips in bars and everything was glamorous. I know I should have been thinking about our career but what really had me jumping up and down was that I could finally go to a diner.

It was all incredibly thrilling. We flew in directly via Los Angeles – and we stayed in the Spence Manor, a hotel on Music Row, which is the epicentre of all the wheeling and dealing that goes on in Nashville. I'd been singing a tune called '16th Avenue' without actually knowing that it was a real place, and now we were walking along it.

Of course, after our first day there, after the flight and the excitement and a few meetings with publishers and industry types, and the jetlag, I was totally fried. We all were. Still, we were in Nashville, and this could turn out to be our only visit Stateside so Nash, Worm and I decided that we'd go out that night while Mum and Dad, wisely, opted to stay back at the hotel. We ordered in some Chinese – ordering in was a novelty – and scanned the gig guide to see who was playing.

The pickings were slim: the only name that we recognised was a guy called Edwin McCain, and we only knew him from a chance spotting on *Letterman*. But we were determined to see something so we fronted up to the Exit/Inn, quite a famous venue, ridiculously early. After some time this guy walked out on stage. He was a cool-looking dude, if a bit short, wearing his guitar rock star low, stupidly low. At first I thought it might be Edwin McCain. He had a three-piece band, a sort of a rock band, and when they started playing it was all heavy, hard, aggressive guitars, more folk-rock than country. Straight away I was hooked. It was as big a moment for me as seeing Lucinda play in Adelaide.

Musically, this mystery guy's songs weren't much like mine, but there was some clear connection between what he played and what I listened to. He wore his heart on his sleeve, like all my idols do, and was singing it like he really lived it, which, by the look of him, was probably the case. I liked his Tom Waits-like whispery voice, the way that he stared at the floor throughout the set, didn't bother talking to the audience and came across as pretty surly. He was the anti-me. What I was most stunned by was that he was young, just 20, the same age as me, as I found out later. So I could add him to my list of young people who were into the kind of music I was – which so far was Bec and Kym.

Again, it was the way the lyrics were in sync with the music which got to me, just as it had with Lucinda. He sang a number called 'Irrelevant', which was about the end of a relationship – how he felt irrelevant – and the mood he created when he sang took it beyond the million other love-and-loss songs you hear every day.

I learned from the woman on the door that the guy's name was Matthew Ryan – commonly known as Ryan. Nash and I don't always agree on music but he liked him too – mainly because he wasn't country. And Worm got enthusiastic about anyone I was enthusiastic about, so we all agreed this was the Next Big Thing.

During Ryan's gig, Nash had gone to the bar, and he thought he'd heard someone calling his name. But as we didn't know anyone there, he figured he was delirious from jetlag and ignored it. Then, when we went back to the bar after the set, a music publisher who we'd met with earlier that day came over and re-introduced himself.

'I thought that was you,' he said. 'Nash, I actually called out to you earlier on.' So this was the voice. 'It's a shame you didn't hear me,' he continued, 'because I was sitting here with Mark Knopfler and I wanted to introduce you guys. But he had to leave.'

Three jaws collectively hit the ground: Mark freaking Knopfler! The guy who wrote one of the first songs I'd ever performed in public, 'Walk of Life', and another of my musical heroes. And a big Matthew Ryan fan, as we found out. We were kicking ourselves: we'd seen maybe the greatest concert of our lives but missed out on meeting the guy from Dire Straits.

We headed back to the hotel, still totally high from the gig, and Nash crashed out, while Worm and I stayed up, drinking, having a ball. In the early hours we realised we were starving, and that all the shops and restaurants and even room service was closed. The only option – and it speaks to our friendship that both of us thought of it – was the remains of the takeaway Chinese that I'd half eaten before going out – which now sat stone cold in the rubbish bin. After a while of pretending to look for other options we dug out these half-eaten spring rolls and leftovers. Unfortunately, someone had dumped the contents of an ashtray in the bin, so before chowing down we had to brush off ash and specks of dirt. There we sat, half drunk, exhausted, eating ash-coated cold Chinese food. Somehow it seemed the right way to end a monumental day.

But it wasn't quite the end. I was so excited from Ryan's gig that I wrote a song before going to bed. I'd written many songs by now, but 'Things Don't Come Easy' felt different – like the first song I'd written in my own voice.

When I was back home in Australia, I kept checking to see when Ryan's debut album, *Mayday*, would be released, but it seemed to take forever to reach record stores. It must have been a year after first seeing him play that I finally had a copy of the record in my hands. Nash and I got together to have a listening session, but I suddenly felt very anxious.

'Have I built this up too much?' I asked Nash. 'How can this record live up to my expectations?'

Thank God I was wrong – the record was brilliant, and it's still among my favourite albums of all time. I'd never heard songwriting like it. Ryan's lyrics were cryptic and dark, more like poetry. I don't respond to poetry, either writing or reading it; I always want a melody to go along with the words! But this was different.

I even loved the *Mayday* album cover. There was Ryan, standing outside this average suburban house, white picket fence and all. He's wearing this cool-looking jacket and shirt, but his hair is messy and a lit cigarette is hanging from the corner of his mouth. And he's holding a hose, watering the garden! It's slightly ridiculous, making him look like some suburban guy coming off a bender. The cover shot summed him up so well.

We had lots of 'only in America' experiences in Nashville. Nash and I were asked to dinner by some people from the record label Almo Sounds, who were interested in the Dead Ringers, and the country record producer Garth Fundis. 'You should meet this band that's coming to dinner,' they said casually, without telling us it was the group Garbage. Nash, who was consumed by being a producer by this point was stoked to hear we'd be having dinner with Butch Vig, the drummer from Garbage, who had also been the producer on one of our favourite records, Nirvana's *Nevermind*.

During dinner I sat next to the lead singer, Shirley Manson, and mentioned to her that we had been at the ARIAs the year before when Garbage presented an ARIA and our band had won Best Country Release. She turned to me and asked: 'Were you the girl with the big silver shoes?' And it was me. My silver shoes had some Australian fame as I'd worn them for a *Black & White* magazine shoot, where I was shot walking down the main street of a remote outback town in the nude with just a feather boa on, startling the locals. Now they had Nashville cred too.

It was a perfect, fun night with good company and the most expensive meal I've ever eaten. This was quite a few steps up from Chinese straight out of the bin; it cost hundreds and hundreds of dollars. At the end of the night, Nash and I thought the polite thing to do was offer to pay for our share, but luckily the label people just laughed. 'No, we pay for you,' they explained. They didn't end up signing us, but Almo did spring for dinner.

I took very little interest in the business end of our trip – one of the good things about having a family member like Nash or Mum as manager is that Dad and I could leave the boring bits to them and trust them to do what was right. I went along to meetings with the rest of the family and afterwards we'd discuss what had been said, most of which was advice to move to the US if we wanted a deal – no thanks, as much as we were loving America we didn't want to live there – and to try and fit somewhere in the mould of what was commercial at the time: Shania Twain, Garth Brooks and LeAnn Rimes. The fact that we were a family band played in our favour – family being a big thing in country music – but once again our lack of belt buckles, pedal steel/fiddle combos and ten-gallon hats made us weird.

It was strange – people constantly told us on that trip, and on others, that they loved how we were doing things our own way – and then they'd turn around and try and make us do things the way they wanted. I think having four of us to talk decisions through really helped us hold our ground; it's a lot harder to remember what you believe when there's only one of you being talked at by persuasive industry people. And some of what we heard was probably good advice – it's just that it wasn't the right advice for us.

We saw the less pretty side of the industry when I endured the strange experience that is co-writing. This is standard procedure in Nashville: strangers are brought together in a back room in some publishing company's office and are left alone to come up with a country-pop masterpiece – ideally in a few hours. One of my co-writers was Mark Moffatt, a terrific guy, an expat Aussie guitarist and producer, who was probably best known for working with Yothu Yindi and Tim Finn (and Keith Urban, later on). The other member of our trio was an Irish guy named Jimmy Stewart.

This Jimmy character was completely inflexible: he'd come up with a line and Mark and I would try and suggest something but he'd shut us down every time. 'No, that's it,' he said. 'That's how the line is going.' I can safely say that it was the worst songwriting experience of my life and the only thing worse than scratching the song together was the fear that someone might actually record it.

I guess it shouldn't have come as a surprise that with the amount of money being made in Nashville, it had turned from the place of innovation it had been in the 1960s and '70s into a conveyor belt. You could still see great things there – Ryan was proof of that – but you also sense the giant machine in action, a machine that tells you what the market wants and then tries to make you fit it. It was so different to the way we worked, which was to write a song, consider if we liked it and then play it.

And yet, everyone we met in Nashville wanted to be in the industry; the waitress who was a singer, the taxi driver who gave me a demo. Our lack of ambition stood out like a sore thumb.

I can see why we didn't get a record deal – they would have been crazy to sign us, a stubborn, unknown band based in Australia! At the time it felt a little disappointing but then again, we just didn't want success in America that badly – we had no interest in getting sucked into the Music City machine.

8

'I don't care if it takes five years or 20, I'll find an audience for your music'

So you just drive, Mr Baylis
Don't you worry about the weather
We're only halfway through our journey
But I think we're gonna make it.

Lyrics from 'Mr Baylis'

Soon after that first American trip in 1996 all our lives changed, in quite a major way. After more than 25 years of marriage, Mum and Dad were breaking up. There wasn't some huge rift or angry explosion; they were the textbook example of a couple that just drifted apart. They rarely argued, but in the latter days of the Dead Ringers, over a period of a couple of years, there was this obvious tension between them that started to have an impact on us as a band and a family.

I think it was partly the result of going through so much, with such intensity, together: the Nullarbor, Southend, the band, us kids. They'd changed as people and those changes were more apparent when they were no longer together. But because they'd had such a good marriage for 20 years, it took some time to realise it no longer existed. Towards the end, my dad was involved with another woman. Not that I approved of it, but I knew that wasn't the catalyst: like I said, Mum and Dad simply grew apart.

I can't imagine anyone not liking my mum or dad; they're very soulful, likeable people that others love to be around. But they didn't want to be around each other any more, to a certain extent.

We were all in Avoca when they came clean and told us of their plans to separate, but it was hardly a revelation. Nash and I were their children and their bandmates; how could we not feel the anger and tension that had crept into their marriage? Strangely – and this is another testament to their strength as people – I think their split did more damage to the band than the family. But at the time, none of us really cared about the Dead Ringers. While the band eventually folded, we emerged a stronger and, I think, a better family unit.

'How do you feel about this?' Mum and Dad asked me and Nash, during our sit-down in Avoca.

'Relieved,' I replied. 'I'd much rather you be happy apart than unhappy together.'

'Thank God. Finally,' Nash added.

Nash is the most practical person you will ever meet in your entire life: his world is black-and-white. He likes living like that. He's a smart guy; he could see that they'd done everything they could to try and save their marriage but now they had to concentrate on moving forward and finding happiness apart. I realise that I'd also been waiting for the day they'd decide to get on with their lives rather than try to save something that was dead.

That's why in the end it wasn't so sad for Nash and me. Even though it broke our hearts at the time, we didn't want to see our parents hurting. I was never fearful of losing them, I knew that however they worked things out, they were both a part of my life and Nash's life.

But I can't pretend it wasn't an incredibly difficult time for all of us. For a while, Mum and I went to Norfolk – we got a visa to live on the island, which you need if you stay longer than 30 days – and stayed with Kurt's family. Being in the close unit helped heal both of us. A few people on Norfolk thought that Mum and Kurt's dad, Jap, had hooked up – we were all living together, after all – but they had a different kind of relationship. What they needed from each other – what we all needed from each other at that time in our lives – was friendship and stability.

If there was an upside to all of this, it's that I was witness to my mother's amazing inner strength. She must have been falling apart at the time and I wouldn't have blamed her for some angry or bitter feelings, but instead she concentrated on making sure that she and Dad would stay friends and that Nash and I would feel secure. She's no victim; she looked after herself as well. But her ability to look beyond the petty and the vindictive with a generosity of spirit – that really shone through in the way she handled the split and eventual divorce. And beyond that, she seemed to grow. For so long she'd been Mrs Bill Chambers, our mother, everyone's best friend – and now she began to emerge as a person in her own right – Diane.

I once wrote in some liner notes: 'To my dad, who taught me everything I know about music. And to my mum, who taught me everything else.' It really is like that. Dad and I had this obvious connection: it's about music, and I love that, and I have learned most of what I know about music from him. But I've become more of the person I am because of what I've learned from my mum.

While we lived on Norfolk, Mum and I took up our little cleaning business again, working in the hotels there. The Dead Ringers were over; there was no way to keep the band rolling in the midst of all that upheaval. But sooner or later we all had to think about making a living – with music if possible.

Over the years there had been various suggestions about the line-up of the Dead Ringers. Some of the producers we'd met with had proposed that Nash and I spend more time up front. It didn't suit Nash; he was now thinking much more about being a producer. I'd ended up being the front person much of the time – basically because no one else was keen on it. And there had also been suggestions that I think about a solo career. Greg Shaw, who discovered Keith Urban, had come to see us in Avoca and said he'd be interested in managing me.

I was on the fence about it. Part of me was really uncomfortable with going out on my own. I loved being on stage with my family.

I loved this little thing we had going. The thought of not having Nash or Mum or Dad with me just terrified me. I didn't have stars in my eyes at all – and I still don't if you want to know the truth. I was a kid, out front of this band that was getting popular, and I was having a ball. And we were having heaps of fun before things went sour between Mum and Dad. The only work I had to do was singing on stage and learning the songs. I was the tagalong that got most of the recognition. Mum, Dad and Nash did all the hard work. Why would an unambitious teenager like me want to mess with that?

I had thought in the back of my mind about one day making a solo album. There were songs I'd written, like 'The Captain', which I knew instinctively weren't Dead Ringers songs, and I'd put them aside with the idea of recording an album by myself. Dad did some of his own recordings so there was already a precedent. But that was very different to becoming a solo act.

As I mentioned, I tend to try and push problems aside. Instead of working through them sensibly, I let them boil over in my head. I was doing a bit of that through this whole period. I couldn't work out what I should do – go solo, which felt so daunting – or think about getting some sort of proper day job, which was even worse! And I was burdened by an awful sense of responsibility – if I didn't keep going with the music, what would happen to my family's income? But if I did, I'd be way out of my comfort zone.

Two things saved me. One was Nash, who in his practical way told me that he was thinking about getting a studio and producing full-time – and that he and I should work together. Believe it or not one of my major worries at this time was who would do my books if I launched my own musical career? I was hopeless at maths; I couldn't imagine being responsible for money. Nash assured me that Mum could still take care of that – and Dad could still play with me no matter what happened. I could make a solo album – and it would be just like making a Ringers album – except that I'd be in charge.

The second thing was Tony Harlow. Tony is an Englishman who had come to Australia to run EMI Records. In a complete coincidence, or one of those happy accidents that have made up my life, Tony had called us at just the time that Nash started shopping me around as a solo artist to various companies. He left a message on the answering machine saying that he'd seen the Dead Ringer Band at the Gympie Muster, which we'd played several times since our debut there in 1992 and he liked what we were doing.

'I don't know if you're looking for a deal or what, but if you're not, then this call is just to tell you I'm a fan,' Tony said. 'But if you are, maybe we could talk.'

Coming from the MD of EMI, a big wheel in the music industry, this was pretty flattering. When Nash spoke with other labels, he'd usually hear back from someone ten steps down the corporate ladder. But Tony was the boss, the head of the company, and he had called us personally.

There was something about Tony's manner which impressed all of us. He wasn't offering us the world on a platter or setting out a ten-year plan; instead he seemed interested in hearing what we wanted to do. He sounded very genuine, totally real.

When we met Tony at his offices in Sydney, he turned out to be much younger than I was expecting; in his mid-30s then. I hadn't met many MDs but I had formed a picture of what executives look like and it wasn't this young and 'normal' looking, almost clean-cut guy who enthused about the music we liked: Neil Young and Gram Parsons and Emmylou Harris. He was a music fan and he knew what he was talking about, so it was like he spoke our language. There was no 'Hey, I'm going to make you a star!' bullshit. Nash told him that our next project would be my solo album and that we had decided to put Dead Ringer Band on hold, and it still is, really, more than ten years later.

We'd had enough experience with the 'music biz' by then to become cynical – perhaps overly cynical – and we were in the habit of running a series of questions by the reps we met to see how they responded. Any sort of weird vibe and we were gone. With Tony we asked him what direction he could see me heading and he shook his head. 'What I want you to do is go away, make the best album you possibly can, then bring it back to me,' he told us. 'Then I'll find a market to sell it in. I don't care if it takes five years or 20, I'll find an audience for your music. I will make it fit.'

I want to give Tony credit for seeing the kind of people we were. I don't think it's a suck up to say that a good record label or a good executive needs to figure out what sort of artist they're working with – and he got us right away. People will say, 'Well he was saying whatever it took', but the point is that other people didn't even do that. And it wasn't as if it was all over the minute we left his office either; we've stayed friends even years down the track when I am no longer with the label and neither is he. He took a chance on us and he was willing to let the record we made be the record it was before even attempting to sell it. Not many people in business – in any business – are that open, or perhaps that crazy.

I had no idea whether EMI was better or worse than Universal or Sony or the rest of them. As we later found out, EMI wasn't in great shape. It was an industry joke that the initials stood for 'Every Mistake Imaginable'. Tony had been hired to turn that around. He was the right guy for the job; our decision to sign with EMI had nothing to do with money or power or promises, it had everything to do with Tony.

So I had a label deal and we had a new chapter looming before us. But before that kicked in there was another big event on the horizon.

For some time since Mum and Dad split, and throughout much of our early days on Norfolk, Mum had been planning a six-week-long African safari. She wanted to go on a big trip and she didn't want to go somewhere we might go with the band, like America. She wanted a separation from music.

I couldn't let her go alone – though on reflection she was much more capable of looking after herself or travelling on her own than I was. It was decided that we would travel together through various countries on her tour. It would mean a long separation from Kurt, but it was another chance to go overseas, which I always enjoyed, and to a non-Westernised place this time, which made it exciting.

Part of the reason that we chose to go to Africa and not, say, Disneyland, was that we wanted to experience something totally new and hopefully have our eyes opened to the way other people lived. We wanted to learn something and be moved by the experience rather than do the tourist thing and drop our money on a shitload of souvenirs. And that's exactly what the trip did for us, although not quite in the way I'd expected.

Just before leaving home, I decided I'd take a guitar along with me. I didn't want to take one of my good ones, so Dad and I trawled the local pawnshops, eventually finding this beat-up old guitar in a shop in Gosford. It cost 80 bucks. Soundwise, it was the worst guitar ever made, but I thought it was kind of cool-looking. There was a painting on it of a cowboy sitting by a campfire, which I liked. As soon as I saw it, I just had to have the thing. Dad and Nash paid for it; they said it was my going-away present. It travelled with me throughout Africa, in this soft guitar case. It would come in handy.

Mum's and my trip wasn't some glamorous, upscale safari. If anything it was the bargain basement version, roughing it in tents, eating simple food that we prepared ourselves. Mostly we slept in camping grounds in wildlife parks, all the time aware that some potentially dangerous wildlife was nearby. Fortunately this way of living was pretty familiar to us – tents were a luxury compared to swags! – although the surrounding scenery was way different to the Nullarbor.

Our driver was a man named Bill Baylis and we travelled with him and Mary, the guide. In the group were 20 of us from all over the place: Germany, the UK, South Africa, Holland and New Zealand, plus some other Aussies. During the six weeks we crossed six, maybe seven countries. I was prepared for some things, not for others – prepared to see terrible poverty, which we did, unprepared to also find so much life force and so many moments of beauty which often brought me to tears. And I was really unprepared to once again see my mother take everything in her stride. She was at ease, wherever we were, whoever we met.

I found out that we weren't the only people at an interesting stage of their lives – maybe that's what draws people to adventures like these. Some nights we'd all sit around drinking and pouring our hearts out. I learned bits and pieces about the other people on the safari: some were seasoned travellers, others were first-timers. It was all so much fun, such a mix of personalities and cultures, which was something I hadn't really been exposed to.

I know I risk sounding as if Africa was some sort of backdrop for my growing pains – it was and is so much more than that. But that trip did feel like my transition from being a teenager to being an adult. I'd been so completely self-absorbed, worrying about my career and whether I'd be okay. Then, as happens with travel, I saw that there were much bigger things in the world – bigger than me. There was so little opportunity for the people we met there, none at all for many of them, and yet everyone was making what they could of their lives. I had sat around feeling sorry for myself; here were people who had nothing and they didn't feel sorry for themselves. It made me realise that I should make more of all the opportunities I had. Just fucking stop whingeing.

I witnessed pure joy in some of the villages we visited. The locals seemed a lot happier than most of the people I knew back home. This was a big reality check for me – I realised how spoiled we Westerners truly are. I saw a little boy who was playing with a plastic drink bottle, which he'd cut in half, added a sail and turned it into a little boat. He was completely fascinated by it. It was the only toy I saw during my six weeks in Africa. I immediately had a flashback to the Nullarbor; that was the kind of thing Nash and I would have done, making do with the little we had.

We whitewater-rafted down the Zambezi, which was a blast, although not something I'd do again in a hurry. I also rode an elephant for the first (and maybe the last) time. The thing bolted and scared the shit out of me, to tell you the truth. We also visited a park in Botswana where, if you're lucky, you can see elephants in the wild from very close range. We were told, however, that it wasn't guaranteed, but as soon as we rounded the first corner – the group was in the back of a flatbed truck – there was an elephant, standing in front of us. It was an amazing moment; this huge, strangely beautiful beast was only metres away. There were tears in my eyes, and I wasn't the only person in the group who felt this huge burst of emotion. Incredible.

There are times when I go into songwriting mode and it comes out of me – music and lyrics – without any apparent reason. Africa was one of those times. I was writing songs as we travelled – and I often had the chance to play and sing. At one village we visited, some kids danced for us and it was a fair exchange that I play – so I sang 'The Captain'. A few nights earlier I'd sung it to the group, around the campfire, and everyone said they liked it. So now I sang it to the kids in the village, and they seemed genuinely thrilled. The children approached me and touched my beat-up guitar, like it was somehow magical. It was a big moment for me, and for the whole group. 'The Captain' was adopted as our theme song.

And I wrote 'Mr Baylis' for our driver Bill, whose birthday fell when we were travelling together.

In the back of my mind there was still the question of what would happen when I got home. As great a time as we were having I did want to go home; I suffered terrible separation anxiety from Kurt, Dad and Nash. I found it hard to mention Dad's name without bursting into tears. I remember sobbing to Dad on the phone, when I did manage to get through: 'Just because I'm crying doesn't mean I'm not having a great time. I'm really enjoying myself!' It all came pouring out.

But I also knew I'd soon be leading the way for the family for the first time in my life. Despite all my good intentions of growing up and becoming a responsible adult, I wasn't quite on top of that. Which might explain why I had my first full-blown anxiety attack on our way home.

The tour ended in Kenya, and we were scheduled to fly home via Johannesburg and Perth. But after we cleared Customs in Jo'burg, we found out that we'd missed our connecting flight, because of a delay with the airline. Nowadays, I'd just accept it as one of the typical hassles of air travel, but for some reason I flipped out. We were stuck in Africa for two more days, which was when the next flight to Australia was due, but because we'd been through Customs, we were now officially in transit. We were stuck in this strange no-man's land, the Twilight Zone. Mum and I were told that we had to stay in a hotel that was specifically for people in our situation.

I lost it completely. I was hyperventilating. I couldn't breathe. Anybody who saw me in that airport must have thought something really strange was going on. Mum had to hold me and physically calm me down, I was in such a bad state. Eventually we got to the hotel. I cried for about half of the stay, and sunbaked for the rest. I came home with a tan, so it wasn't all bad. (Spoiled brat? Yeah, probably.)

It was like a repeat of the old sleeping disorders but during the day this time. An eerie feeling of being scared of nothing in particular, or maybe just the result of not owning up that I was scared. Being tired and emotionally overwhelmed didn't help either. But it wasn't the end I wanted for the trip that had opened my eyes to so much. I still wasn't in the best shape when we finally got back to Sydney, and Dad and Kurt collected us at the airport.

Other things came out of the experience too, though. On the most basic level it was a reminder of our good fortune and Mum and I were determined to share it. When we got back we both got involved in charities like the one run by Geraldine Cox, who does such good work with orphanages in Cambodia, and in the Christina Noble Children's Foundation in Vietnam. We have stayed involved with those charities to this day.

I didn't go straight back to Norfolk on my return. Instead I spent a few days on the coast with Dad, Kurt and Nash. It was great to be with them again, even though I knew that there was some hard work ahead of us. But even then I didn't have these huge expectations for my solo career. I had no clear plans for the future, really, apart from one day having children. The best I could have hoped for was that music would help me provide a living for the rest of my family – Worm included, of course – and pay back Mum and Dad for all the years they'd provided for me. They'd carried me for long enough. And no one outside of the country music world knew who I was, anyway.

I figured that if I continued to play this style of music I'd never be hugely popular. I'd certainly never get played on mainstream radio. And that was okay, I didn't care. I knew that was how it went. This wasn't America; I just didn't have a shot here with the type of country music that I played. In fact, I probably didn't have a shot in America playing this music either, so it was something of a losing battle. But I was stoked that Tony Harlow liked what I was doing and had given me a chance to make a 'proper' record and then do a tour. That was enough.

9

Going solo

Well I don't have as many friends because
I'm not as pretty as I was
I've kicked myself at times because I've lied
So I will have to learn to stand my ground
I'll tell 'em I won't be around
I'll move on over to your town and hide.

Lyrics from 'The Captain'

After all of my reluctance and fear, the odd thing about making *The Captain* was how much I enjoyed it. One thing I've found is that thinking about what I do in terms of 'career' scares me and turns me off – or it did until I learned to come to terms with it. But when it comes to the creative side – writing, singing, making decisions on titles and song lists and cover shots – I'm very confident and clear. I felt I knew exactly what I wanted on this record.

Nash suggested – and I agreed – that we should record the album on Norfolk Island. It was the place where I felt the most comfortable, and that is such a big part of making records. Kurt and his family would be nearby, as would Mum, and Dad was going to play on the record, as well. Tony Harlow thought it was a good idea, too, if a little bit out-there. The one catch, however, was that there wasn't a recording studio on Norfolk Island (portable home studios were still a thing of the future). But Nash came up with a solution for that; he suggested that we make our own studio. He already had all the gear he needed back in Avoca, so he organised to have it flown out to the island. Easy.

When it came to deciding where we should set up, the Menghettis stepped in. Jap had previously run a restaurant on the island with his late wife, Sue, but it hadn't been used for a long time. All the catering equipment – the kitchen, cutlery, crockery, everything – sat there, gathering dust. We'd adopted it as a sort of clubhouse, a place to hang out, and Jap agreed to let us use it as the studio. It was less than a kilometre away from where we were all living, so it was ideal. We started recording there in late 1998.

The whole crew came out to help with the record: Worm, BJ, Jeff McCormack – who pretty much engineered the entire album – and Dad. Mum was there, of course, making all the food, taking care of business, being Mum. It was more than making a record; it was a way of sharing my Norfolk experience with my friends and family, over the course of about a month.

I can safely say that I never felt alone during this entire period, something I feared as much as anything else. My parents were getting divorced now – although it would be years before they formalised it – yet soon they'd be touring and travelling together.

Maybe that's weird, but not in our family! They'd started to become good friends again, which was a wonderful thing to witness.

The whole time we were recording, local people would drop in and have a listen to the songs. The Governor of Norfolk, Anthony Messner, turned up unannounced one night. Norfolk musos would also swing by, like Wayne Pendleton or Pendo as he's known. We'd met Pendo on that first trip to Norfolk and he had become one of those instant friends for life. When we were recording he would often bring treats like champagne, caviar and single-malt Scotch. To pay for the spread, he would draw extra shifts at his various jobs. He didn't mind, that was just the Norfolk way. In fact, it was Pendo who got me into Glen Livet, my favourite drink. He convinced me that a quality single-malt whisky was good for my voice. Maybe, maybe not, but I definitely thought I was a better singer after a couple.

Aside from the constant power short-outs it was a perfect way to make a record. True, Nash had to improvise quite a bit on site – I ended up recording most of my vocals from the toilet, a sort of ready-made reverb unit. There was a belief that the site was haunted – I don't know about that but I wouldn't go down there alone at night, because the flickering lights would freak me out, just a little. Sometimes there was a strange, hard-to-describe feeling to the place. But it did give the record a real sense of place. It sounded very much like Norfolk to me. Still does.

Nash and I worked well together with the shorthand we'd developed over the years. The other musicians would speak up and give their opinions about this or that – I couldn't work with people who don't have opinions about music; it would feel as though they don't care – but when it came to the major decisions, as I say, I was confident about making them, sometimes in consultation with Nash, sometimes alone.

There were very few arguments but there was creative evolution, as there is with any project. I'd written 'The Captain' as this very simple folk song, with just one acoustic guitar and my vocal. But Nash heard both that song, and another called, 'Don't Go', which I co-wrote with Worm when I was 14, a little differently. In the end, I went with the band on 'The Captain' and kept 'Don't Go' as just voice and guitar. I tend to perform songs exactly the way I write them – I've learned over the years that I don't have to stick so rigidly to this rule! Most of the time, though, when I sing live I do 'The Captain' as I wrote it – without the band.

While we were working on the album, I told Nash the story about writing 'Mr Baylis' for the driver in Africa and he asked me to play the song to him. When I did he said it had to go on my album, which I wasn't sure about. 'It's a birthday song,' I said, 'it even has this guy's name on it.' But Nash felt strongly enough to convince me.

Our faith in Tony Harlow was borne out during this time. Normally during the making of an album someone from the record company 'drops in' to see how things are going but Nash dug his heels in and said, no, this is our part, making the album, and they agreed – I'd say largely because of Tony's influence. We pretty much gave them the finished product. In fact, hardly anyone from a label has heard a record of mine before it's finished. We've always had full creative control. And that's a beautiful thing from an artist's perspective. I was very lucky, especially for someone making their debut album.

On the album were the brilliant Buddy and Julie Miller from Nashville. I'd long been a fan and had been fortunate enough to sit in with Buddy when he came out to play the Byron Bay Bluesfest in 1998, which to this day is one of my favourite events, a festival that nothing – not even pregnancy, which has twice been the case – will stop me attending. As Julie Miller doesn't travel, Buddy had needed a female singer to help him out on stage at Bluesfest. I'm not sure how he heard of me but he emailed and asked whether I'd be interested in the gig. Can you imagine? That was the best and worst news of my life: Julie Miller is renowned for her beautiful, heart-stopping harmonies, now I'd have to step in her shoes; that scared me shitless. But it was such an honour that I couldn't possibly say no.

I'd learned the songs and when I met Buddy in Byron I learned that we would do one rehearsal together in his hotel room on the day of the gig. All musicians have their own way of working and these guys were used to winging it, which is the opposite way to how I work. Fortunately, Buddy is one of the nicest guys on the planet, so he made it just that bit easier for me though it didn't help that halfway through our rehearsal Steve Earle, who was also playing the Bluesfest and was sharing a band with Buddy, came walking in.

Physically, Steve is a big bear of a man and has a presence that can't be denied – he doesn't just quietly drift into a room. Keep in mind that this is the country music outlaw who wrote 'Copperhead Road' and dozens of other great songs, a former drug addict who's done time in jail and has been married seven times (and counting), twice to the same woman. Of course I'm a massive fan, but I was trying to be so cool about it. Steve grunted hello; the guy's no hugger, that's for sure, and offered me one of the chicken chips he was eating from a packet. I hate chicken chips but if Steve Earle is offering, you don't have much choice; I smiled, ate it, hated it and kept quiet.

The rehearsal made me feel better. Buddy told me that Steve was going to come on stage and sing during his set, but I was so keyed up I didn't think much about it. I didn't realise that when he came up to sing he was going to share my microphone. Was this not the greatest moment of my life? After the gig, Steve came over and said that he had some shows coming up, and he had this duet on his new record, a song called 'Poison Lovers'. Did I know it? Could I sing it? Well, I didn't know the song, but I wasn't going to admit that.

'Yes, yes, I do, I know it really well,' I stammered back.

'Great, let's do it tonight,' Steve replied.

Shit! I raced back to my hotel and played the song over and over, learning it as best I could. So I ended up singing both nights with Steve, as well as playing with Buddy, a dream come true.

That scored us a spot on the next Bluesfest, which is a hard gig to get if you're a nobody. Peter Noble, who runs the festival, took a punt on me and has since become another massive supporter. I've played there ten times, which I've been told is the most appearances by a woman (my book, my brag). Best of all, Buddy Miller had told me that if I was ever in Nashville and needed anything, to simply get in touch. So when I thought of who I wanted on my first solo record, I thought, wouldn't it be great if I could get Buddy and Julie.

Nash and I – and Kurt – flew to Nashville, to Buddy's house, where we recorded several songs, including 'The Captain', with Julie singing harmonies. Although they were among my musical heroes, they were great people, who made us all feel totally relaxed and welcome. Cats scampered about everywhere while we recorded, and these beautiful guitars decked the walls of their studio. It was really homely.

The first song we did with the Millers was 'These Pines', which I'd written about Kurt and Norfolk while I was on the road, in a hotel room in Esperance, WA, suffering Norfolk withdrawal. From the window I had been able to see some Norfolk Island pines dotted along the beach, which reminded me of the island. Buddy sang harmony on this one, and his singing actually reduced me to tears. Then when Julie leaned over to me and said, 'You guys blend so beautifully together. I think I like the blend even more than Buddy and Emmylou,' my perfect day was pretty much complete.

During the break when Buddy took us to his favourite restaurant, a nearby Chinese place, the waiter brought out some fortune cookies. I cracked mine open with a real sense of anticipation – after all, I was in musical heaven, there had to be a sign. I pulled out the slip of paper and read the words 'You love Chinese food'.

By the time everything was done, I was wildly excited about the record. I wanted to go out and shout from the rooftops: 'This is my first solo record and I'm very proud of it.' I was very precious about the title of the album. We had a meeting with EMI and I said, 'The album is going to be called *The Captain*.' Everyone there, even Nash, said, 'Okay, but we might throw some other ideas around.' 'No,' I said firmly. 'That's the name and that's all there is to it.' It was very uncharacteristic for me, but I was hell-bent on it, and it was never mentioned again. I knew that song was the glue that held the album together.

The other thing I always take full control of is the cover shot. On *The Captain* I wanted to look like a singer-songwriter; I wanted to look good but not sexy; I wanted substance. It's my favourite cover shot of any of my records. I'm sitting in a gutter somewhere in Sydney, outside a photographer's studio, wearing a second-hand black velvet suit. I've got my hands up, almost as if I wanted to hide behind them. I do look a bit vulnerable, but at that moment in time I was pretty comfortable being that person.

My experiences promoting the record, especially early on, were a mixture of the brilliant and the bizarre. I was learning more than

I could ever have imagined about the music industry and meeting a lot of new people, some of them highly respected musicians, who I was clueless about. I was from the country music world, not the pop or rock side of things, and I had little idea what people looked like or where they fitted in or what my place was in all of this. In retrospect, it was good to be a bit naïve, otherwise things could have gone to my head at this point. Well, okay, things did go to my head, a bit, but my family and Worm were always there, ready to bring me back down to earth.

Just before *The Captain* was released I came down to Sydney with a whole group of my Norfolk buddies. Worm was there, too. We booked a cheap motel room in the city and went out – the Norfolkers were only in town for one night, so we decided to make the most of it. It was a big night for me; we went to Kings Cross, loads of different bars, strip clubs, everything. I'm not much for clubs – partying isn't my scene and it almost killed me – but I was excited about my album and just wanted to let my hair down. I even danced, and trust me, I am not normally a dancer. At around seven in the morning we stumbled back to the motel, cooked up a massive breakfast and then everyone crashed wherever they could find a spot.

I don't think I'd been asleep for an hour when my phone rang. It was someone from EMI, who told me that there was an unofficial, industry-only gig tonight for Neil Finn, at the Bridge Hotel in Balmain. They felt that as the label's new signing I would be the ideal person to open the show. But I had no band, no guitar and, crucially, no voice. I was shattered from the big night and though I knew Neil Finn was with Crowded House and they had a big hit at that time called 'Better Be Home Soon', I didn't know him. So I passed, hoping that I hadn't offended anyone.

Minutes later my phone rang again. This time it was someone higher up at EMI, telling me that I really should do the gig. I politely passed again.

Soon after that, Nash called.

'This is an important gig,' he said. 'I think you should consider doing it.'

'Nash,' I whispered, 'I hear you. But it's not that easy. I'm hungover, over-tired, I have no voice – and there is no way I could do a gig by myself. Ever.'

I'd never played totally alone. At the least, I'd always had Dad playing guitar with me. I hated the idea of standing up and playing by myself, especially in the messed-up state I was currently in. But if Nash was calling, I started to get the idea that maybe it was a bigger deal than I thought – and probably a bit early to blow my career with EMI.

'Hey,' I asked Nash, 'why is this so last minute?'

Nash went on to tell me that Tim Rogers had been booked to do the gig but just called and pulled out. I didn't know who Tim Rogers was beyond being the lead singer of You Am I, but at that moment I was pretty cross with him. 'Fuck Tim Rogers!' I said to myself.

Still, I didn't have the courage to pass on the gig a third time, so with my head throbbing, I started to think of who I could call to help me out as a backing band. Dad was out of town, he couldn't help, so I rang pretty much every player I knew – Kym Warner, Chris Haigh, James Gillard, Jeff McCormack, among others – but without any luck. Then I started calling back-up singers – they could wail a different song, I didn't care, as long as someone was there with me – but again I struck out. The best I could do, after dozens of calls, was to borrow a guitar from Sam Hawksley, a Sydney guy, who also had a gig that night and wasn't free to play. But even then it was a large guitar, way bigger than the small-body, custom-made ones I was used to playing. My worst musical nightmare – standing in front of an audience on my own and falling to pieces – was about to come true, and I had no way to stop it.

At the gig I was the surly, reluctant one; the rest of my Norfolk friends, who were keen to see Neil Finn, came along, sat in the other bar and got drunk all over again. Worm, the trouper that he is, carried the loaner guitar for me and held my hand as I wept and moaned before the gig. 'I can't do this,' I repeated in my croaky voice, 'I can't do this.' Worm kept telling me I'd be fine, yet being alone absolutely, totally, freaked me out. But now I had no choice but to play. Or at least try and play.

Well, this kind of story is usually accompanied by a fairytale ending, but I can tell you now that my set was even worse than I imagined it would be. I was fucking awful. The room was full of journos and industry people, who all seemed in good spirits, at least until I started playing. I played more wrong chords than right ones. The only good thing was that no one cared or listened after the first few notes. Everyone proceeded to talk through my set, which usually pisses me off, but on this night was a blessing. But it was so bad that I cut my set in half and walked off, humiliated, embarrassed. As I was pushing through the crowd, with my head hung low, trying not to cry, this tall, rumpled guy stopped me.

'Hey. I'm Tim Rogers,' he said. 'How are you? Do you mind if I borrow your guitar? Thought I might do a few songs after all.'

I could have beaten him over his rock star head with my borrowed guitar. He'd put me through the worst gig of my life, and now he not only turned up, but wanted to 'do a few songs'? Tim may have been this great singer-songwriter, or the biggest rock star in the world – whatever – but on that night I totally hated him. He blew out the gig, turned up anyway, borrowed my borrowed guitar – I was fuming. I don't even think I acknowledged Tim: no hello, good luck, go fuck yourself, nothing. I had to get out of the room. I handed him the guitar, which wasn't even mine – hope that was okay, Sam – and walked away.

Over the years I've gotten to know Tim and have since discovered that he is a really special guy, a beautiful soul, who I have so much time for. If only we'd started out better. But he and I do seem jinxed in terms of live gigs – some years later I was asked to sing with You Am I at Homebake. The song was 'Heavy Heart' and I felt quite nervous about doing it – I love other people singing with me, but singing with someone else, particularly a rock band with a loose cannon like Tim at the head – can be hard work.

I learned the song – and then Tim said they were going to do it with different timing. Disaster. I sang it the way we'd rehearsed it, but the rest of the band went with the new timing and the result was a horrible mess. Shane, who I was married to by then, told me at first that I had just made it worse in my own head – then he saw it on a YouTube clip and had to tell me that yes, it really was as awful as I'd thought! Luckily I could laugh about it by then.

Thankfully, finally meeting and singing with Neil Finn, which I did soon after *The Captain* was released in May 1999, was a way better experience. It was at an EMI conference in Port Douglas where I was booked to play. I had recently recorded Neil's song 'Better Be Home Soon' as the B-side of a single and when I was introduced to him just before the gig, he mentioned that he knew about that. I told him that some people had requested it but I couldn't play it on guitar, so I couldn't do it today. 'That's okay,' he said, 'I'll help you out and we can sing it together.'

In my naïve way I just thought he was a great guy – which he truly is – I didn't think that it was a big deal to ask Neil Finn to help me out on guitar – and for him to agree.

Of course it was great, a real moment. It's such a sad song yet I couldn't wipe the smile off my face – all the way through I was saying to myself, 'Stop smiling, you look like an idiot. Look sad, look sad!' Neil's music wasn't what I had grown up listening to. I didn't know him as 'our Neil Finn' – if I did, I probably wouldn't have dared to ask him to help. But as a musician, playing with him was a wonderful experience on its own.

Okay, one more name-drop. My meeting with Paul Kelly was a little different. I did know Paul's music – really well. I'd seen him play when I was in my teens, when the Dead Ringers were on the road. We all went along to his Gold Coast gig on a rare night off and since that night, Paul was someone I've always looked up to: he's an amazing re-inventor, making different types of records, doing what appealed to him rather than following trends or fitting into any one category. I totally respect that. He's had major success on his own terms and he's built what seemed like the dream career to me. Paul had the success and became a household name, without all the celebrity crap.

He walked up and introduced himself at my first Bluesfest; he said he'd caught a couple of songs from my set and was really impressed. I was stunned, speechless yet again. Paul asked what I was doing next. 'I'm off to see Ben Harper,' I replied. He said, 'Yeah? I don't really get Ben Harper,' and walked away. Paul Kelly doesn't humour people just for the hell of it. I love that about him.

It was around this time that I had my first close encounter with Bernadette – Bern – now one of my closest friends, although it would still be some time before we actually met. Okay, let me explain. We're both mad-keen AFL fans. As I later found out, the first time that Nash, Worm and I went to the MCG to see an AFL game, in September 1999 – we'd seen plenty of games in Adelaide, but your first time at the 'G' is a special occasion – Bern was also at the game.

That clash between the Blues and the Essendon Bombers was memorable; we were down by 11 points at three-quarter time, and then went a further six points down at the start of the final quarter. But thanks to my very loud and hopefully inspiring cheering, and with maybe a little help from Anthony Koutoufides, the Blues dug deep and won the game by a point, in the process making it into the final. (Best not talk about what happened the next week against North Melbourne.)

Little did I know on the day that Bern was sitting close enough to us to hear my barracking; it'd be a few more years before she'd meet and marry Worm and become part of a '2 friends for the price of 1' deal. (They now have two boys, Townes and Banjo.) Like Worm, Bern is a real cut-the-crap type of person, someone who can see straight through all the hype and bullshit that comes with what I do.

Of course, getting out there and selling *The Captain* wasn't all about meeting and befriending musicians that I respected (or otherwise). Undergoing a 'promo wheel' taught me plenty about the music industry, and not all of it was positive. I was proud of the record and wanted to talk about it, so I agreed to pretty much everything. But I soon learned that certain parts of promo suck.

I was starting to pick up the signal from people around me that radio airplay was crucial for a successful record. Radio can often make the difference between a mildly successful record and a smash hit. I didn't see my songs as being 'radio friendly' anyway. Still, the label would set up times when I could go into radio stations and meet the staff and play in front of them to try and get them interested in the record. And it was just horrible. Everybody sat on their hands; the silence was deafening. I felt like a performing monkey. I thought to myself, 'This is so not for me.' Then they'd wheel in the next act who'd have to go through the same charade.

I was still young, but I'd played to enough audiences to know when I was making a connection. And for much of the promo wheel – especially the times I played to radio staff, I knew that I was not connecting with these people, or at least I wasn't connecting with their 'format'. However, after another fancy dinner courtesy of the industry, I'd see the upside, as I've always tried to do. While they probably wouldn't play my song, I'd just had a great meal I could never afford on my own, and I'd met some nice people. I'd had a good chat.

There were some breakthroughs: Triple J played the song 'The Captain' a little bit, which was quite something, given I was seen as a country artist and they were a rock station, but again I didn't realise how significant that was. Because I never listened to the radio (I still don't), its power was a bit lost on me. Again, simply from not knowing the world I was stepping into, I missed things. When we launched the album at The Basement in Sydney, people were coming up before the show, telling me that so-and-so was in the room, and I'd pretend to know who they were talking about. The truth was that I had no idea. I knew I was supposed to be excited, but I didn't know how important a record launch was, or how influential these people could be. Probably a good thing as I might have blown it. As it was, everything felt really good on stage.

I developed some great relationships with the people at EMI, from Tony Harlow down; people such as Cathy Oates, Graham 'Asho' Ashton, Tom Inglis, Nicole Richards and Melita Hodge, who ended up co-managing me. Chris O'Hearn came back to EMI not long after we signed. Leon Concannon was the country guy, the one who tipped off Tony about us, and who started the whole thing rolling. Everyone, particularly Melita, put their hearts and souls into our little project. I was there all the time; I'd drop in to their Sydney office just to say hello, I liked the people so much. I would hang out and talk music with them. Working and getting to know the people at EMI was such a great experience.

EMI did their best for me, even shielding me from any bad press. The first review that I read, which they initially tried to hide from me, was from a Brisbane street press mag, for the single 'Cry Like a Baby'. It read: 'And you thought Shania Twain was bad. This song will leave you standing in the corner saying, "Make it stop, please make it stop", as the men in white coats come to cart you away.' Very encouraging, huh? But it was kind of funny to me. I wasn't offended. I didn't really know that reviews could be so powerful. I just thought that everyone gets good and bad press, and I was glad to get any.

But things improved after that. Media started to find my whole 'family saga' intriguing; it got to be a real talking point. 'Your dad's in the band? Your brother produced the record? Your mum does the merch desk?' Everyone wanted to talk about that stuff. 'You lived on the Nullarbor? You hunted foxes for a living?' It was an awakening for me, the first time that I genuinely realised my upbringing was perhaps a little bit different to the norm. I'd never stopped to think about it before.

Somewhere along the line I started to grow into my personality. Going to things like Bluesfest helped – in Byron, I looked pretty normal, even straight. Elsewhere I stood out, just because I was this young woman playing a type of music that young women didn't usually play – at least not in Australia. I was developing my own style that could mean looking like a hippy one day, wearing a top hat on stage the next and going super fashionable on the third day. I discovered that it was empowering to be a bit different, to not fit completely in. When there were suggestions, as there were occasionally, to 'style' me or make me look a bit slicker or sexier, I just said No: I knew how to dress myself.

I wasn't trying to be perverse or difficult, I just knew instinctively that it was important to be comfortable with what I was doing. And while I wanted the record to succeed – I definitely didn't want to be the person writing songs in my bedroom for myself – I'd accepted that I wasn't ever going to appeal to a mass market.

As it was, quite a little vibe developed around the album, which was so much more than I had expected. Eventually it would go triple platinum, over three years, so while it never got into the Top Ten, it sold well over 200,000 copies. I didn't make much money from it; labels normally invest a lot of money in a first album and if it sells, that usually just means they earn back their investment. But it meant that I needed to get off Norfolk, in order to seize the moment and also make some kind of living. I was moving on, yet again.

10

Baby makes three

Falling into you carries me far enough away
I just hope that the wind doesn't blow you away.

Lyrics from 'Falling Into You'

As interest in *The Captain* gradually built, Kurt and I began to slowly drift apart. That makes it sound as if the two were related but I don't think they were; though Kurt wasn't always comfortable in my world, it wasn't because he was jealous of my success. He came out with me on the road occasionally, and he enjoyed some of the travel that came with my job, but he was always so dreadfully shy, someone who only ever felt at home when he was at home, back on Norfolk Island. Things were different for me, I loved Norfolk too but my life was taking me elsewhere.

One of the sweetest things from this time was that the people on Norfolk were really proud of what we had achieved with *The Captain*. And I say 'we' quite deliberately. Even though it was my name on the cover and me speaking during the interviews, it still felt very much like a family effort. That was vitally important to me, and went to show that all those concerns I'd had about 'going

153

solo' were pretty much unfounded. I enjoyed going out on tour just as much as I had during the time of the Ringers, pretty much because my family was still involved with doing the hard stuff – management, merchandising, arranging tours and so on – while all the fun things were my domain. I never felt alone, and had plenty of people to share the good times with.

But my break-up with Kurt was inevitable, and I probably did hasten our split a little more than him. It wasn't a messy end; there were no hard feelings, and a lot of love and goodwill remained between us. We were together for about three years; it had been the first serious relationship for both of us. But we'd simply run our course and in the long run I think it was our very different personalities that pushed us away from each other.

I guess that on paper one of the biggest moments for me during *The Captain* period was winning the Best Female ARIA in October 2000. The year before the record had won the Best Country Album ARIA, which, although still a surprise, sort of made more sense – after all, it was a country record. That was when Slim Dusty made his comment about me being totally country, which meant a lot given the resistance to that in some circles. But when it came to the mainstream ARIAs, even getting nominated left me gobsmacked. At first I thought, 'Were there only five girls with albums this year? Why have they put a country artist like me on the shortlist?' I only knew half the artists who were at the awards. I was still living in my own little music world, where I was listening to Gillian Welch, not trying to learn about Oz pop.

It was an even bigger shock to win, pipping higher-profile artists like Kylie Minogue and Vanessa Amorosi. It was a double celebration because Alex Lloyd, who was my labelmate at EMI and a good friend, was named Best Male Artist. But truth be told, the far bigger moment was getting to play alongside Paul Kelly at the awards.

I'd had a really memorable night with Paul at The Basement in Sydney just before the ARIAs. He was playing that night and when I arrived with Dad at the venue Paul was standing by the bar, in the crowd, watching bluegrass band Uncle Bill play their support set. Once again I was struck by his normality. 'How cool is this guy's career?' I thought to myself. 'He's one of the biggest names in Australian music yet he can stand here, watch the band and blend right in.'

After the gig, when the room emptied out, me, Dad, Paul and some of his friends sat around, playing guitars and singing favourites. We played songs by Bob Dylan, Johnny Cash, George Jones and heaps of others. Paul would call out requests: 'Anyone know any Louvin Brothers?' and away we went. Paul had a few of his friends there, and at one stage Dad and I were playing this Louvin Brothers song when Paul grabbed this woman and danced while we played the song. It was such a lovely time. My song 'I Still Pray', which I wrote soon after, was directly inspired by that night. Paul was playing a lot of gospel at the time and I figured, 'If it's good enough for him, it's got to be good enough for me.'

I had been asked to play at the ARIAS and I brought up the idea of Paul joining me on stage. I was really thrilled when he said yes, and especially so when he agreed to sing 'I Still Pray' which we'd eventually record together. As I stood there on the ARIAs stage, singing in front of all those people, I was thinking, 'That's my dad, and, shit, that's Paul Kelly.'

I remember at the after-party, one of the guys from the band Frenzal Rhomb told me it was his favourite moment of the night. I looked at him and said, 'Really?' Weird. Punk rockers liked me?

A few days later, I collected a prescription from my local chemist. There was a note attached to it that read: 'Kasey, congratulations on your ARIA. We are all very proud of you here at the Avoca Surgery. PS: Your pap smear is overdue.'

I sang again with Paul Kelly soon after, during one of my first headlining shows at the Metro, and that was another massive experience. He was playing elsewhere in Sydney that night, but agreed to come down for the encore, which I had listed as 'I Still Pray' – that song got a real workout! In typical form I was both excited and worried – that the crowd wouldn't ask for an encore. I'd be the idiot who had Paul Kelly standing backstage and couldn't win over a crowd enough to get him out front.

Thankfully, we did get called back for the encore. I went out and sang the first verse, which is the way the song goes, and Paul simply walked out on stage – I didn't introduce him, because, frankly, most of my crowd would be fans and could spot him a mile off. Then this amazing thing happened: the crowd absolutely erupted. The noise was so powerful that I felt as though I was being physically lifted into the air. The intensity almost scared me, to be honest. I lost my place in the song. Afterwards, I was speaking with Worm, who had been working the lights. Worm is a tough man to impress, but he said that he felt as though he was going to be crushed by the noise, it was so overwhelming, so huge.

In 2000, things seemed to be going well with my career. I started work on a second album, which would become *Barricades & Brickwalls*. Nash and I had been back to the States on the strength of *The Captain*'s success, to see if we could line up a deal there. We saw a lot of label heads in Nashville, most of whom seemed a bit surprised that we already had a finished album to show them. One guy from Atlantic even said to Nash that it was odd to be sitting there with people who had a clear idea of where they were going – he was more used to artists asking, 'Well, what would you like me to do?' Eventually we signed with a major American label, Warner Bros.

I was earning a living from touring by now, and after the Warners deal I started playing shows through America and Europe, where we opened for Bryan Ferry of all people. We played in France, and also parts of Scandinavia, places I never imagined visiting, let alone performing in.

We played a gig in Oslo, Norway; the venue was on one level of this amazing ten-storey building. Nash and Jeff McCormack from the band snuck away for their usual pre-gig 'herbal cigarette', and found a bathroom with a fan. 'Perfect,' they agreed. While blowing the smoke into the fan they somehow set off the fire alarm, which meant the entire building – all ten floors – had to be evacuated. They snuck out and blended into the crowd on the street, whispering to us, a bit sheepishly: 'I think it's a false alarm!' We'd also played at the Grand Ole Opry in Nashville, sacred ground for country music lovers, which was a huge thing, especially for Dad.

I certainly wasn't huge in the US – then, or even now. *The Captain* didn't have any obvious hit songs on it so the gigs varied depending on whether a local radio station had decided to play songs from it before we played or not. If I was opening for another artist I would get their audience. And it also helped that, quite by fluke, we got a spot on David Letterman's show.

I watched the show of course and I always tuned in for the music spot. But it didn't occur to me that it was such a big thing until all the phone calls started to us – in the US – from Australian media. I think we probably got more publicity out of the booking than the gig! The actual performance I remember as a bit of a blur. I had the flu and I was worried that I wasn't going to be able to sing once I got out there. I do recall David Letterman coming into the dressing room to introduce himself – and that he was very nice. Oh and Jeff McCormack farted in Dave's chair during sound check. Nice.

All of that was fun and exciting, but as a music fan myself, the best parts of this time were the gigs we got to play and the musicians we played with. For example, when Lucinda Williams asked me to do a charity gig, an industry fund-raiser. The gig was seventh heaven for me: on the bill that night was Steve Earle and his son Justin Townes Earle, plus Ryan Adams, Gillian Welch and David Rawlings, Lucinda, Buddy and Julie Miller, and Matthew Ryan – the guy I'd heard on my first visit to Nashville in 1996. It was as if someone had read my mind and arranged my ultimate all-time line-up. Just when I thought it couldn't get any better, or bigger, Buddy and Julie played a few songs and then said: 'We're going to invite a friend up to play' and on stage stepped Emmylou Harris.

During Lucinda's set she announced: 'I'd like to get my new favourite artist up here to play a few songs for you – Kasey Chambers.' My God! I think I played 'The Captain' and 'This Flower', but I could have played anything I was so starstruck, just floating in space. To make it all that much weirder, I noticed that the actor Donnie Most was sitting in the crowd, so on the one night I'd been in the presence of Lucinda, Emmylou, Steve Earle, Buddy and Julie – and Ralph Malph from *Happy Days*!

Afterwards I was in the bar when I spotted Matthew Ryan. I felt that I had to tell him about that gig in Nashville in '96 and how it changed everything for me about music and songwriting. I went over, introduced myself and spilled my guts and, typically, he kind of shrugged it off, saying something like, 'Oh yeah? Okay.' Then he went back to his beer. But he kept talking with me and, of course, I developed this little 'rock star' crush on him – his slightly dysfunctional personality made me warm to him right away.

We formed a bit of a bond over an evening spent together. It wasn't a date or anything, even though he took me back to his apartment, which does sound a bit dodgy. But there he played me heaps of albums, which I guess was his way of introducing himself to me. I'd asked him what kind of music he liked, because I couldn't pinpoint what that might be and he said, 'This is my favourite record right now', then played David Gray's *White Ladder* which was new at the time. I didn't know about David Gray at all, something I'm embarrassed to admit, and even more embarrassing I thought it was only okay, not quite what I expected. It had loops and samples and a lot of electronic sounds, which I didn't really get. I'd never listened to anything like that and had no great desire to, either. Ryan could see that it didn't work for me, but I kept the name David Gray in the back of my mind.

Ryan was a night owl and I wanted to keep hanging out with him so eventually it was early morning and we were still talking and playing records – or rather he was talking while I listened, which isn't characteristic. He took me for breakfast to some sort of diner and bought me a very American breakfast: a waffle–pancake stack, before dropping me back at the hotel. I think that long day (and night) might have been one of the best music lessons I've ever had. That same day I wrote the song 'Million Tears'.

Kym Warner, my friend from teenage years, had moved from Adelaide up to Sydney and was living in Balmain with Carol

Young, his partner. But for a time Kym was between houses and he came up to Avoca to stay with Worm and me; we were sharing a place. Kym talked about his friend, a guy named Cori Hopper, who lived in the same street in Balmain and was an actor and a music fan. He thought we'd get along. Cori was just about to head down to Melbourne for three months to work in a play, so we invited him up to Avoca, simply for a few farewell drinks, the night before he was due to leave.

Bec, my Dolly Parton-loving girlfriend, had also moved up to the Central Coast and she was over that night. Worm, Kym, Mum and Bec and I were at home, in the middle of playing a board game, when Cori walked in. Certain details stick in my head: I remember I was wearing an aqua blue Billabong top; I was sunburned, as we'd been out on the beach all day, so I looked a bit like a lobster. And I remember that as soon as Cori walked inside, and our eyes met, something hit us both like a thunderbolt. Boom! He's a good-looking guy, with his big dark eyes and striking features, but it was way more than that. I've met enough handsome men to know that this was something else.

We experienced what could only be described as the complete love-at-first-sight cliché. It was a new sensation for me, that's for sure. It was suddenly as if there was no one else in the room; it was almost ridiculous. I swear to you, if I'd seen the scene in some chick flick, I'd run for the exit, trying not to puke. I'm just not into that girlie kind of thing, but this connection hit hard enough to knock us both off our feet.

When the world stopped spinning, Cori sat down with the group, and later on we all went down to the pub. He and I flirted and talked – we talked a lot. I actually can't recall either of us speaking to anyone else, to the point where, towards the end of the night, Kym pulled me aside. 'Hey,' he joked, 'you've stolen my mate away. I was supposed to be saying goodbye to him.'

Kym had been right; we did get along. Cori and I are very alike, both of us are outgoing, talkative, positive, cruisey people who would run a mile from any type of confrontation. He was a music fan, as promised, and also a big Aussie Rules fan, a West Coast Eagles supporter. We talked about footy a lot though my heart was still with my beloved Carlton Blues. And he was slightly old-fashioned, a real gentleman. Cori and I fell deeply in love pretty much from that first meeting. It was remarkable, something that I didn't think happened in real life.

The next day Cori put off his flight to Melbourne for as long as he could, and headed down to the beach with all of us. Despite my sunburn, he and I sat in the sun and talked for maybe eight hours, barely stopping to notice anything or anyone around us. Bec was there, too. When Cori finally said his goodbyes, Bec turned to me and knew, straight away, that I was gone, totally in love. She could see it in my eyes.

From then on it was a case of mutual obsession. Our phone bills grew huge as we constantly called and texted each other. I flew down to Melbourne a couple of times, and he came back to Sydney when he could, and I was actually relieved when his play's run was shortened. He came straight back to Avoca, and moved in with me and Worm. And that was fine, because I wanted him around me all the time.

I was a love junkie, for the first time in my life. Mum was stoked, too, because she now had another surrogate son to care for. Cori got along really well with her, and showed a lot of respect for people, something I appreciated, and a quality that other people seemed to admire in him, too. Everything seemed to work out so perfectly.

Of course, it's not ideal for a country singer to be blissfully in love. We're supposed to suffer all of life's dramas and heartaches and then write about it in our lonely room, but instead I was floating several feet off the ground. I actually mentioned that to Cori one day, not long after he moved in. I'd had 21 years to write my first record but now it was time for the sequel and everything was all wrong, but in the best possible way.

'How the hell am I supposed to write songs now that I'm so happy?' I said. 'That's not the mindset you're supposed to be in to write country songs!'

Cori's answer was, 'I'm sure there's enough country music in you to make a happy song sound sad.'

He was right, too, because I went away and wrote 'Falling Into You', the last song I came up with for *Barricades & Brickwalls*. On the surface it sounds like a sad song but listen closely and you can tell I'm beside myself in love.

It sounds crazy I know, but almost as soon as Cori moved in we began talking about having children. Not straight away, of course, maybe in a couple of years. We felt so right together that it seemed perfectly natural; becoming parents was definitely part of our plans. We felt it was just meant to be. And Cori was very comfortable in my world, as I was in his. He clicked straight away with most of the people at EMI that I dealt with all the time – Melita, 'Asho', Tony Harlow. He was now part of the group; when anyone talked about me, they were also talking about Cori.

I spent a lot of 2001 travelling between Australia and the USA, while working on *Barricades*. In March of that year I got the opening slot on an American tour with the cult singer-songwriter Robert Earl Keen. Robert, who is huge in the US, had written songs that were recorded by the country 'super group', the Highwaymen. He was quite a rootsy artist, a storyteller. I was excited to get the tour, we all were; what could be better than working with people you respect and admire? And as a songwriter, I figured that his audience would be into what we were doing, and would be quiet and attentive.

It was around this time I met Canadian Fred Eaglesmith, another of my favourite singer-songwriters. I told Fred about our forthcoming Keen tour and was a bit taken aback when he looked and me and said, 'Oh, really?'

'Is that not good?' I asked. Fred went on to explain that opening for Robert Earl could be pretty tough, but left it at that. And this from a guy who's fronted every audience imaginable! My ears pricked up immediately. If Fred found it hard, I thought, what chance was there for me?

As I was about to find out, there are certain rites of passage every singer must go through. On the alternative country trail in the US, there is the rite of the Robert Earl Keen tour. I didn't meet Robert at first – which is not that unusual with support acts; often the main artist just stays in his or her bus, and even more often, they don't know who you are; you might have been picked by their managers. I definitely make it a point to pick my support acts after one really bad experience, but it depends on the artist. But I met his band and they all seemed like nice guys, welcoming and friendly.

Our tour started out in Baton Rouge and we were then scheduled to head to New Orleans. The first gig was well attended; there were maybe 500 people there, a good-size crowd for us to play in front of, as we were still finding our audience in America. But this wasn't the quiet crowd we were expecting; it was young fraternity kids from the country, college kids out for a wild time. This was not a listening audience. They loved Robert Earl Keen. And they certainly didn't give two shits about me. About three songs in, through a rendition of 'These Pines', a chant started: 'ROBERT EARL KEEN! ROBERT EARL KEEN!'

If I'm opening up for someone I know I'm not going to get as long on stage as if I was the main act, so I tend to skip the long, story-song ballads, for a punchier set. And as Americans tend to enjoy the Aussie accent, I throw in a few stories about the Nullarbor. It's all about winning people over in 40 minutes, at least in theory. It sure didn't work that night. Somehow we made it to the end of the set, but I think there was more applause when we left the stage than there was while we were playing.

If I had been a few years younger, I would have panicked, but I came off stage feeling challenged rather than discouraged. 'I will win over a Robert Earl Keen audience,' I told myself. I decided not to resort to snippy comments or sarcasm, which would probably be wasted on them anyway. 'I will win them over!' First we needed to tweak the set, and replace anything even vaguely slow with up-tempo songs like 'We're All Gonna Die Someday', which usually got a lively response. It'll get better, we all agreed, last night was just a bad gig. Forget about it, move on.

So we travelled down to New Orleans, determined and ready to play. But we'd overlooked the fact that it was Mardi Gras. The venue was much smaller this time, and almost as soon as I opened my mouth to start singing, all these tiny beads, which are everywhere during Mardi Gras, started raining down on us. It was the same audience of drunk frat boys, just a different city, and this time they were armed! Someone nailed Dad's guitar with a beaded necklace while he was playing the Beverly Hillbillies lick in 'We're All Gonna Die', knocking it way out of tune. It sounded awful, just terrible. Everything went wrong. It was like being in a war zone and we couldn't wait to get out of there.

Our American tour manager, Greg 'Greggles' Wilkinson, stayed relentlessly upbeat through it all: 'How'd it go, luv?' he'd say as I came off stage to another chorus of ROBERT EARL KEEN! 'Bit of a hard one? You'll be right.' And fortunately, things did better as we went further north and the crowds changed from frat kids to more what we were expecting. The one thing I had going for me was that women rarely opened for Robert and that gained me a little more respect. His band told us we were doing really well, and that it was often much worse for their supports. Some couldn't even get through their set, let alone the tour.

The promoters were clearly expecting us to quit at a certain point. Phrases like 'If you last the tour …' crept into their conversation. But I didn't feel personally wounded. Apparently the same thing had happened to Emmylou Harris during a festival, when she was playing before Robert, and she is an American legend, so it was more to do with a particular set of one-eyed fans.

During my set at a gig in Carrboro, North Carolina, I spoke with the audience – a much kinder audience, thankfully – and told them what had been happening: the chants, the drunks, everything. Jokingly, I said I'd really appreciate it if they could start up their own chant when Robert came out on stage. Which they did, yelling: 'Kasey Chambers! Kasey Chambers!' at the top of their lungs as he played. Robert even got us up on stage with him, so he saw the funny side of it. It worked out well for us in the end. It became like a quest, a challenge. It wasn't a total disaster. We were travelling America, playing gigs – we were up for anything we could get.

In total contrast, my next US tour was a dream trip: five weeks opening for Lucinda Williams. First, Lucinda had personally asked us to support her so the atmosphere was much warmer and more welcoming, but also, I connected with Lucinda's audiences more than I had with Robert's. And it meant getting to see her for free every night.

I got to know Lucinda pretty well, as I played with her on this and other gigs. She's regarded as a difficult customer by some people who've worked with her, and she is rigorous about what she does – sometimes she'll even stop a song because it doesn't sound right and go back to the beginning – while live on stage! But as a person, I like her a lot. She is surprisingly open – even a bit girlish sometimes with her cute giggle. I responded to her mix of worldliness and fragility.

On the first day of the tour she knocked on the door of our bus. I casually answered the door, but inside I was as nervous as hell. Holy shit, it's Lucinda! She smiled and said, in that gentle drawl of hers, 'Can I borrow some nail polish remover?' 'This,' I thought to myself, 'is just about the greatest moment of my life.'

One night, she and I were out in a bar in Nashville and I asked her about a guitarist who she'd famously fallen out with. She started talking about the falling out and as she talked, she began crying. Everyone in the bar would have been aware she was there – but she was so caught up in her story she tuned everything else out and I found her naturalness attractive. I could tell she'd done some hard travelling but she'd managed to retain some innocence as well.

I missed watching just one show during the entire tour, and that was only because we had an early-morning radio gig the next day. And, could you believe it, that was the night she got

Elvis Costello up to sing with her. I must have some sort of Elvis Costello curse, because I was on the same bill with him at the Newport Folk Festival (now sponsored by Dunkin Donuts, according to the T-shirt I still have somewhere). This was a famous event, where Bob Dylan had 'gone electric' back in the mid-1960s. I was seriously jetlagged, so I decided to have a power nap before Elvis's set; I was very keen to see him play. That nap became a heavy snooze, and when I woke up I raced to the stage, just in time to hear the man say: 'Thanks for coming, goodbye.'

In September 2001, towards the end of another Australian tour, I was in Queensland, on the day of the AFL grand final. As a diehard footy fan I planned to be in front of a TV come start time, to catch the game between Brisbane and Essendon. We'd become friendly with the guys from the band Speedstar, who were also signed to EMI, and we got to watch the game at the home of Ben, one of the band members. But even though I was excited about the footy, I was just feeling off all day, a little sick, in a weird, unfamiliar way.

Fortunately I was on my way home. But even when I was back at Avoca I kept feeling ill. It then hit me that I was a few days late for my period. But there was no way I could be pregnant, right? I was on the pill, for one thing, although my timing got all messed up while I was in America. Still, I hadn't been with Cori for the few weeks I was on tour, so the notion that I could be – gulp – pregnant, just didn't make any sense. Possible, but unlikely.

I guess I should have seen the signs: throughout that Oz tour I was getting the strangest urges. Pasta salad became a real obsession with me. Every day I'd insist we stop at a supermarket and I'd buy these big tubs of the stuff, which I'd spread on bread and eat as sandwiches after the gig.

'Okay,' I said to Cori, 'let's buy one of those pregnancy tests, just so we can rule that out.'

So we did just that. Back home I breathed deeply, went into the bathroom, peed on the stick, as you do, and waited to see what the result was. A few thoughts were running through my head, mostly the fact that *Barricades* was just about to be released, and perhaps this wasn't the ideal time to fall pregnant. And Cori and I had been together for less than a year, so maybe we weren't ready to have a baby just yet.

But all those concerns disappeared as soon as I looked at the stick. We were pregnant! Cori and I were beside ourselves with joy. There were no reservations, no fears – we were jumping-up-and-down thrilled. Cori's desire to start a family was just as strong as mine.

I was due for an interview with Richard Wilkins and a crew from Channel Nine to talk up my new record. Richard had to miss his big scoop, I had this amazing news, but I wanted to tell Mum and Dad and Nash first before the rest of Australia got word, so I sat through the interview with a goofy grin on my face. All I'd ever really wanted to do in life was have a baby, and here I was pregnant, yet I wasn't in a position to tell the world. I certainly didn't want the whole of Australia to know the news before my mum!

So we told out mothers first – Cori's in Perth – and Mum in person. They were both thrilled. It was the first grandchild, on both sides – how could they not be excited? No fears, no concerns, just unconditional joy and support. Mum knew that our love was rock solid, even though we hadn't been together long.

And then we told Nash. In some ways, Cori was just as apprehensive as I was, but not about the baby – what was he going to tell Nash? 'Er, I've knocked up your sister, just before her new album comes out'? Although he is my business partner and manager, Nash is my brother first and was equally delighted. And Dad of course felt the same. There was unconditional support from everyone.

'But what about the record?' I asked Nash.

'It'll be fine,' Nash said, 'we'll work around it.'

Maybe inside he was thinking, 'Fuck, this could ruin everything', but he didn't let on. He was very cool, as was Tony Harlow, who had a little boy of his own and knew how important family was to me. Not one person in my circle gave any indication that my pregnancy was a problem, which was the way I wanted it because at that moment, despite the record on the horizon, my accidental career was at best a second priority. Hearing my music played on the radio was wonderful, but it didn't quite compare to the sensation of a baby growing inside me.

11

'I am so not pretty enough!'

Am I not pretty enough
Is my heart too broken
Do I cry too much
Am I too outspoken?

Lyrics from 'Not Pretty Enough'

Making *Barricades* had been a blast – and again, I had gone in
with a clear idea of how things would work. I wanted to show the
many different sides of me this time, musically and emotionally.
It was a very conscious thing to start with the upbeat title track
and then move into 'Not Pretty Enough'. I wanted to switch from
sounding strong and confident to a more vulnerable mood, and I
tried to keep that going throughout the record.

I got to record with some great people: The Living End, who
I had seen open for Green Day in Chicago (and blow them off
the stage), seemed just right for 'Crossfire' because that song is
so different to others on the record and has a guitar break their
guitar player Chris Cheney was perfect for; Paul Kelly sang on 'I
Still Pray'; Lucinda on 'On a Bad Day', a dream fulfilled, and for

a second time, the great Buddy Miller on 'Runaway Train'. I also recorded 'A Million Tears' with Matthew Ryan, which was a real highlight as my musical crush on him had been the inspiration behind that song. I didn't give him much direction apart from telling him that he could do whatever he wanted, and Ryan came up with this great, gruff wailing vocal, almost spoken.

I didn't worry too much about the possibility that all my 'guest stars' might somehow take over the record – the more guests the better, I figured. I thought it was the time to capitalise on the opportunities of recording with these amazing people. After all, it might be my only chance.

Worm chipped in again, too. The song 'Barricades & Brickwalls' was his idea and literally a road song. When we were touring, we still travelled as we had in the Ringers days and Worm and I would always room together because we both liked watching TV all night. In my house the TV is always on – I can't relax any other way – and Worm is the only person who can bear it. And on the road, Worm, Dad and I would all cram into a crappy van we used – we'd ride up front and all the gear would be loaded into the back. We were driving back to Avoca from somewhere when Worm said that he had an idea for a song. Worm doesn't play an instrument, doesn't sing, but he understands music far better than he thinks he does. He spoke the line out loud: 'Barricades and brick walls won't keep me from you.' We liked it straight away, and wrote the song driving along in the car.

As for the album's 'hidden' track, 'Ignorance', that came about from an interview with a US journalist, a guy named Dan Dunn.

He said to me, as we finished our chat, 'If you're not pissed off with the world, you're just not paying attention', and the phrase stuck in my head. We arranged for all the royalties from that song to be paid to the Christina Noble Children's Foundation, the charity I'd gotten involved with soon after our trip to Africa.

Once 'Not Pretty Enough' took off, its lyrics assumed an importance that they didn't have at the time I wrote it. I knew it was a different song in some way and when I first played it to Nash I said, 'If I ever get a song played on mainstream radio, this would be it. Probably won't, but if there was ever a chance, this would be the one.' But I didn't think it would be that big – and although people say it seems obvious now, you have to remember that this was the era of Britney Spears and Shakira – put that song up against one of their tunes and it certainly doesn't shout 'Commercial Hit'!

Nash knew it was a strong song, but typically he didn't get over-excited about it, or anything else, for that matter. Whenever I played my songs to Dad, he always told me this was my best song yet and when I played them to Nash he would think about what could make them better; he was on the lookout for quality control. You need both sorts of people in your life.

I wrote 'Pretty' as a song about feeling invisible. I had had success on my own terms with *The Captain*, but it was obvious that out in the music industry there was only one path for most young women; over-sexualised and over made-up. To succeed you needed to look like Britney or Shakira. Eventually there would be a backlash as people started to question if they were such great role models for young girls which I guess was why the song hit a chord. To put it in a nutshell, a lot of people – women – wanted to be Britney, but they felt as though they were me, Kasey.

I later found out that Slim Dusty and his wife, Joy McKean, were fans of the song, too, because, as Joy would say: 'We never expected to be regarded as "pretty enough". The setbacks were the same for all of us, though in different eras. We could relate.'

When we made the video for the song, I was starting to show, just a little, so Cori and Ryan Renshaw, who were shooting the video, came up with the clever idea to have me sing while sitting down and simply shoot me from the neck up. And it worked really well, I think. (If you look closely at the clip you might spot Angus and Julia Stone, who were brought in as extras, and have since gone on to have their own successful music careers.)

From the minute we knew about the pregnancy, Cori and I completely got into the idea of nesting. We took the prenatal classes, read the books, saw the scary videos, and our excitement over-rode everything. We had a midwife, whose name was Linda, that we got to know really well during the prenatal classes. She was someone we'd felt comfortable with pretty much from the word go, which was a huge relief. I couldn't care less about the potential hassle of labour.

When it came to being a parent, Cori was right in step with me; he wanted to learn everything, to the point where I had to ask

Me (in red) and Beccy Sturtzel, now Beccy Cole, a great friend and inspiration, and today a hugely popular country singer. I wrote my first song, 'Beccy', in her honour.

My band, The Brown Smelly Shits. That's my friend Kym Warner, me, Beccy and Nash from left. It didn't catch on.

The Dead Ringer Band: me, Nash, Dad and Mum. I guess we didn't look like your average country band, which had both advantages and disadvantages. One well-known entertainer said we'd 'never work in this business again' after we toured with him.

From left: Chris Haigh, Dad, Bryan de Gruchy, me, Mum, Nash and Pete Drummond on the drums. Chris later played with us in The Lost Dogs; Bryan made instruments that we all played and loved.

When we didn't have a room booked on tour— which was most of
the time — we'd set up a swag by the road and camp there.
We'd also sometimes hunt food for dinner.

The Dead Ringers with our first and only ARIA, for Country Release of the Year, 1996.

My dad, Bill Chambers – fox hunter, guitar picker and the key musical inspiration of my life.

Dad, Mum, me and Nash playing in Warnervale, NSW, May 1994. Are they Ozzy Osbourne's glasses?

Yep, that's me, walking some outback street in the nude for
Black+White magazine. The locals were shocked, to say the least.

With Kurt Menghetti, the first 'serious' love of my life, who I met on Norfolk Island.

Norfolk Island, the place and its people, played a huge role in my life. It's where I recorded my album *The Captain*.

Below, from top left: Worm, muso and friend, Wayne 'Pendo' Pendleton, Dad, me, Kurt Menghetti, Nash, Camille Te Nahu (who sang on 'Not Pretty Enough') and Mum.

I ride an elephant with Mum, for the first and probably only time, in Africa in 1998. Scared the heck out of me.

Visiting a school in Malawi with fellow traveller Claire while on safari. Later on I played my song 'The Captain' for the students — and they seemed to like it!

Me, Paul Kelly and the bluegrass band, Uncle Bill. Paul is another huge influence and someone whose career I'd love to have.

With the legendary Steve Earle at the Byron Bay Bluesfest 1998. Steve offered me chicken chips. I hate chicken chips. But who refuses Steve Earle?

Hanging out with Lucinda Williams at the Bluebird Café in Nashville, while promoting *The Captain*. Since I first saw Lucinda sing when I was 16, she's been a massive influence.

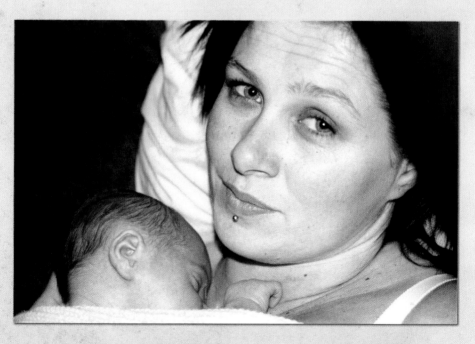

This shot was taken soon after my beautiful baby boy, Talon, was born on 22 May 2002. The epidural really helped!

As a baby, Talon got to meet some famous folks. Here he is with me, his dad, Cori Hopper — and Bert Newton ...

Rove McManus ...

John Farnham ...

Bryan Brown ...

Matt Damon ...

and Jay Leno.

Shane and me on our wedding day, at home, Christmas 2005.
We didn't tell any of our guests that we were getting married.

Shane and me taking our vows, with Worm, my Mate of Honour, and
Shane's brother Steven looking on. I promised to cook Shane slow-roasted
red wine shanks at any time. I keep some in the freezer, just in case.

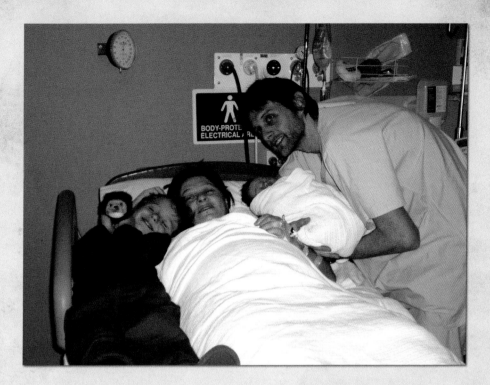

Tal, me, Arlo and Shane on the day of Arlo's birth, 15 July 2007.

Arlo with his namesake, American folk-singing legend Arlo Guthrie.

Arlo with me and Shane at his first gig,
our band The Lost Dogs, Avoca Beach
Hotel, August 2007.

Didn't someone say never to work with kids or animals? Did I listen?
That's Dad (aka Poppa Bill), me and the little hillbillies: Talon,
Townes, Skye, Arlo, Jake, Tyler, Bela and Eden (from left).

Shane and I were lucky enough to take home five Golden
Guitars from the 2009 Country Music Australia awards,
held in Tamworth, for our album *Rattlin' Bones*.

I'm excited! January 2011, and I've just won the Single of the Year gong again at the CMAAs, for 'Little Bird'. That song felt like 'Not Pretty Enough', but through the eyes of me today, a woman in my 30s.

him to stop reading the how-to books for a while. You would have sworn that he was carrying the baby. I put on a lot of weight, which didn't worry me at all. I could eat whatever I wanted! Everything seemed so glowing; even morning sickness. Cori would come in and check on me, and I'd have my head down the toilet, saying: 'I'm great, I'm great!'

It was around this time that I first met Shane Nicholson, whose album Nash was producing. Nash was starting to work with other people now, like Troy Cassar-Daley and Jimmy Barnes. Shane, who is fussy – shall we say! – about his production was working on his first solo album, called *It's a Movie*. He was from Brisbane so he had come down and was sleeping on the couch at Nash and his partner Veronica's place while they made the record. He's so quiet that I didn't notice him much – or even have a conversation with him for a while; he was simply a new person in our little group, someone who I got to eventually like as a mate and whose musical career I admired.

Barricades was released in early 2002 and I was feeling so great I said I was happy to do whatever I could to promote it. Cori and I even did a nude photo shoot, with me very pregnant, for no other reason than it seemed like fun, which ended up on the cover of *HQ* magazine. I felt no embarrassment about being as large as I was, and Cori is the kind of guy who doesn't need an excuse to lose his clothes, so he enjoyed himself, too.

There had been no huge expectations for the album beyond the fact that it earn back its investment. EMI, Nash and my then co-manager, Gary Rabin, worked hard at getting some radio time for it – and they were up against it at first. I remember one mainstream radio station saying – definitively – that they would not play any song of mine as I was a country singer. I also remember that when 'Not Pretty Enough' started getting airplay, they were forced to give in. Can I gloat? Just a little? Ha, ha, ha ... And once the album did get that radio exposure, I was able to sense that it would become much bigger than *The Captain*. You could feel its momentum – and also people started coming up to me for the first time on the street to congratulate me or to say they'd enjoyed a song.

It wasn't as if I became Beyoncé – there were no paparazzi at my door, no breakfasts with Mick Jagger. The nice thing about having success in Australia is that we're not good at putting people up on pedestals; we still expect public figures to be just like us. In the US, I've seen stars with their fans and the relationship is about one saying 'May I touch you?' to the other. Here, people would come up and say: 'Your song got me through my divorce'.

And the thing I've found is – you can largely choose whether to chase celebrity or not. I certainly enjoyed some bits of fame; it was fun to get made up and wear nice clothes when I had an album to promote. The occasional bit of star treatment – like getting flown over to the States to do a fashion shoot for *Rolling Stone* magazine – was fantastic. The rest of it – going to the opening of every envelope – just was not me. At one stage, when I was hugely pregnant, Cori and I went to a movie opening to see the new *Star Wars* because he's a fan. There was a red carpet and a whole lot of people walking down it, most of whom were famous for being famous. I didn't feel like participating, so we walked around the back, avoiding the cameras. We got to enjoy the free movie and we didn't have to do interviews to earn it!

Just before *Barricades* was released, Tony Harlow wrote me a touching, very personal note, where among many other kind things, he said something that perhaps I should have thought about more closely. (It would certainly come back to haunt me in a few years time.)

'I always feel you have to be very careful to call it quits before you stop having a good time,' Tony wrote. 'I know it can be hard to say no when you're asked directly – an artist who's reached your level might now need someone to say "no" more than to say "yes". This is just a thought you might consider.

'I'd like to say that we want you to enjoy the process of working on this record' – he was referring to *Barricades* – 'and I'd like you to call and talk if you feel this is getting out of hand. We are paid to ask more; sometimes we can manage perfectly well with less if that's better for you.'

Tony also wrote this:

I realise that you are always exceptionally generous in speaking kindly about your record company, sometimes more than we deserve, I'm sure. I do, however, know that I'm speaking for everybody here, including myself, when I say that we feel much the same about working with and for you. This goes from top to bottom

of the company, and I think it's remarkable that you've converted
so many people to the music you love. I think it's something only
you could have achieved – and when I hear them talking, the word
'country' never comes up. It's just 'Kasey' and that's a reason to
work 110% in itself. That's an achievement.'

Two things stand out about this letter; one is that I can guarantee very few artists would get a note like it from the MD of their record label. Particularly the MD of a label like EMI. This wasn't some little indie label where caring notes to the talent are part of the landscape. By then Tony would have had an inkling of interest in the new album, and might even have thought that it could do well – but the second thing that strikes me is that he was so perceptive – more perceptive than me about my eagerness to please – and he was willing to protect me from it.

I'm making him sound too good to be true when in fact Tony is very much flesh and blood; he and Nash went head to head more than once – but I do really believe that I owe a lot of my unusual career to meeting this unusual man at the time I did.

So did his letter teach me to start saying No? Not yet. Having gotten through the morning sickness stage of my pregnancy, I was full of energy. I thought I could take on the world and win. I really didn't understand that it might be time for me to ease up.

Before my due date of May 2002, the band and I went back to America for another run of dates. Warners, our new US label, were still struggling to get us radio over there but they had had some traction from an unexpected source; 'The Captain' had played on *The Sopranos* which was the highest-rating show on TV at the time. Snatches of our songs got played all over – ten seconds of some track would appear on *Days of Our Lives* for example, and on other shows. But *The Sopranos* had a big impact, partly because they played a big chunk of the song and also because the show was known for its music. Fans would Google songs from there and find out who had played what. I doubt anyone Googles songs from *Day of Our Lives*.

I still get asked about getting on *The Sopranos*, but the truth is, I'm not sure how we got on – and I've never even seen the segment, or any episodes of the show. The story is that the producer was driving along, heard 'The Captain' on the radio, and decided he wanted it on the show. I like that story so I'm going to go with this version, though there are a few other people who have claimed credit.

One final story about *The Sopranos*. Some time later, when the show won a bunch of Emmys, the producer got up on stage to make a speech. He thanked his crew and cast and then he also paid tribute to all the musicians who had been part of the show, like 'the Rolling Stones, Elvis Costello – and Kasey Chambers'. We didn't know each other, so my name must have just popped into his head, but when I watched the broadcast, all I could think of was the many people around the globe also watching and thinking, 'Who the fuck is Kasey Chambers?!'

For this two-week long US tour, Matthew Ryan, my Nashville mate, opened for us and I continued my musical education under his guidance. While we were in Boulder, Colorado, Ryan took me to see David Gray play – the guy whose record I hadn't really understood at first – and this time it all really clicked for me. I was opening up to different kinds of music, maybe becoming more open-minded about things that I wouldn't have tolerated five years before. The electronic noises now made sense – maybe Dad's training had been holding me back. Strangely, though, Dad also loves Gray's *White Ladder*.

Our second-to-last show of the tour was at a club called Bimbo's in San Francisco. Before we went on I was feeling a bit dizzy and Nash put his foot down, insisting that I chill out for a while before we started the show. A little thing like pregnancy and dizziness wasn't going to prevent me going on. I gradually felt better but we decided I'd do the gig sitting down.

I went out and faced what was probably the biggest audience I'd played to in the States as a headliner. The first three songs of the set were okay, and then I began to play 'These Pines' when I started to feel a lot worse. All I can recall was trying to get up off the stool, because I feared falling forward onto my stomach, possibly hurting the baby. Dad and Jeff McCormack could see on my face that I wasn't right. Dad held me just as I collapsed on stage.

I don't recall much of what happened next. I was lying down backstage, and a call went out in the crowd for a doctor. A gynaecologist, an Australian, just happened be at the gig – what are the odds of that? – and he came back and told me to lie still. I wanted to get back out and play the gig, but he said no, no way.

Typically, I was putting pressure on myself to please the audience. Nash, however, insisted that the gig was over. He went out and said that everyone could have a refund, which nobody asked for. By the time I made it onto the bus, I was back to myself enough to shout at Nash for blowing out the gig.

The people from Warners had been very concerned throughout the tour, worrying that they'd been pushing me too hard. When I collapsed at Bimbo's, they decided the least they could do was bump me up to business class for the trip back home. Because they knew I didn't like travelling alone, they also bumped up Worm, so we both came out ahead. And when I got home, there was a sweet bonus: 'Not Pretty Enough' had gone to Number One on the charts, knocking Shakira off her perch.

A lot can happen in a fortnight, I guess. I began hearing my song on the radio purely by chance, and I was being stopped in the street and the shops for my autograph. It was timing. Pure dumb luck. Whatever, that song seemed to connect with a lot of people. Of course I was just as excited about being pregnant as I was about striking a blow for oppressed teenagers. It was such a wonderful time. I walked around my local mall, Erina Fair, with my shopping trolley, deliriously happy, big as a house, with the number-one single and album in the country. People would do double takes when they saw me.

The song's success also meant I was meeting some interesting characters. When I had the chance to meet Steve Irwin, I brought along my Steve Irwin doll, hoping to get his autograph. I was a huge fan. I was waiting outside his dressing room, texta and doll in hand, when he appeared, with this massive python wrapped around his neck. Steve looked at me and said, 'Oh, I am so not pretty enough!' I just loved the guy straight off, it was such a perfect moment. Cori and I co-wrote a song called 'Follow You Home' about Steve. We really admired what he stood for and how he was always himself, totally unaffected, a true Aussie bloke.

I did convince Nash to let me play at Byron, at my favourite gig, Bluesfest, when I was eight months along. No way was I going to miss out, even if the only thing that would fit me was a cowhide print dress. Aside from that though, that was pretty much the end of the line for me while I was pregnant. Our baby was almost ready to join us. Life really couldn't get any better.

12

Tal

You can buy my life on radio
And order me by mail
But not everything about me is for sale.

Lyrics from 'For Sale'

As I disappeared into pregnancy mode *Barricades* continued to sell, eventually reaching seven times platinum, with sales somewhere near 500,000. Not that I was concentrating on sales numbers – when I did find out, I was amazed. Half a million copies! All of this was overwhelming, but it was great to have the time off and concentrate on the really big thing in our lives, our baby. I had this constant reminder of the real world growing inside me. That was far more incredible than a number-one record, even though that was great, too. I never felt any pressure from EMI about promoting the album – and even if they did make requests, Nash acted as my buffer.

Nash had just found out that he and his partner, Veronica, were expecting their first child within a few months of ours, and they were just as excited as Cori and I. And Dad would become a father, again, soon after Nash, so this was a very fertile period for the Chambers family. And Cori and I had been worried that our child wouldn't have anyone to play with!

Four days before I was due, on May 22, Cori and I decided for some reason that we needed a new couch and we needed to go shopping for it right now. I had it in my head that I'd run overtime with the baby; I didn't think it was about to happen, not yet. We went to a furniture store in Gosford, to try out different models. At one point Cori caught me sitting on one and joked: 'Get off that one. It's expensive. If your water breaks we don't want to have to pay for it!' And pretty soon afterwards, I did indeed start feeling a bit strange.

Back at our house a bit later, I still wasn't feeling any real pain and I'd had no contractions. But when I stood up, my water broke – just like that. To me, that was great, because I was worried that I wouldn't really know when I was entering labour, but now it was pretty bloody obvious. Cori called our midwife, Linda, who said to time my contractions and call back.

I'd decided to have a bath before doing anything else, but had a serious contraction almost straight away. The pain surprised me. My next contraction came three minutes later – there was no big gap, and it was as painful as the one before. We called Linda again and although she asked some questions, I couldn't answer her. The pain was so severe.

'Um,' Linda said, as she listened to me struggling to talk. 'Can you put me back to Cori?'

With pleasure, I thought, but was in too much pain to say a word.

Linda told Cori that we should get in the car – now – because we were a bit further along than predicted. Mum was with us by this time. We'd done some dry runs to the hospital, in heavy and light traffic, and figured we needed about 25 minutes to get there.

The drive to the hospital was pretty much a blur, although I can remember, about halfway there, screaming out. When we arrived, the first check showed that I was six centimetres dilated, in my first hour, so I'd barely experienced any pre-labour at all. All along I'd said that I at least wanted the option to use drugs, if the pain was too much, and I didn't need much persuasion to ask for an epidural. But the staff was a bit wary about this: at first they told Cori that I was too far advanced for pain relief. They changed their minds when they realised that the baby was posterior facing. They now needed to slow down my contractions and reposition our little, painful bundle of joy, because a baby facing that way was way harder to deliver.

I'm not an advocate for drugs by any means, but once they'd given me the epidural, things changed. The whole childbirth thing was a breeze. Ten minutes earlier I'd been telling Cori that there was no way we'd ever do this again, but as soon as the epidural kicked in, I looked at him and said: 'Oh my God – we can have another baby!'

When they repositioned the baby, they explained that they'd have to cut me. I turned to speak to Cori and then told them,

'Okay, you can do it now.' By this time they'd already done what was necessary. Man, those epidurals really work.

Then I said to the nurse, 'I'm not in any pain, but I feel like I should push.' 'Well, you must be ready,' she told me. And I was. It was weird; as much as I couldn't feel any pain – you could have sawn off my leg and I wouldn't have felt a thing – I still had this instinctive urge to push. They used the forceps on Tal, but apart from that it was a relatively smooth delivery. It had been only four hours since my water broke.

As our baby emerged, Cori yelled: 'It's a boy! It's a boy!' Then he burst into tears. So did I. It was such a powerful, emotional moment. The funny thing was that our little guy didn't cry, not for ages – all the adults around him were sobbing like, well, babies, and he lay there, quietly checking us out. He was small-ish, weighing six pounds six ounces. And, of course, he was the most beautiful baby on earth. All right, he actually looked kind of funny at first, a wrinkled old man, like most babies, but to us he was beautiful. It really was the greatest moment of my life – our lives. I have such great memories of giving birth. And I seriously believe that if I hadn't gone for the epidural, I would have been that woman you hear down the corridor in the maternity ward screaming: 'Get this fucking thing out of me!'

We'd decided not to find out what sex the child would be until he or she was born, and had picked out two names. Cori had found the name Talon in a fantasy book; it was a character that was part man, part bird. If it was a girl her name would be Willow, something we'd agreed on almost as soon as we found out we were pregnant. We didn't tell a soul about our choices, and kept tight-lipped throughout the nine months.

After making sure Talon was really a Talon – which we decided he was after his first hour in the world – we chose Jordi for his middle name. That was what people called Cori's grandfather, George, who really was a Geordie.

Tal was such a good baby. He had jaundice so we stayed in the hospital for a few days and he tended to sleep a little longer than some newborns; I had to set my alarm to wake him up for feeds. Our blissed-out post-natal state remained in place throughout my hospital stay. Now and again the staff delivered gifts from fans, which was an unexpected surprise. And if we perhaps got a little extra attention at the hospital because of my 'status' – I especially liked the electric bed – well, we weren't complaining about it. Cori slept on the floor each night and Mum swung by each day.

By the time Tal was three months old, we decided it was time to get back on the road. I still needed to work, though I'd make some money from the success of *Barricades*, enough for a deposit on a house – and also I was keen to get back to music.

Mum had said to me that my pre-baby life shouldn't just stop because I had a child, and if anyone understood that work/life balance, it was Mum. It may seem strange to people, but I had loved travelling when I was a kid, and my life, until Tal was born, was all about living on the road. As a baby I had fallen asleep behind the bass amp when Mum and Dad played. That was more normal and more comfortable to me than bringing up a kid in a house in the suburbs. I wanted Tal to be part of my entire life, and I was lucky that I had the type of job that I could share with my son, unlike most working mums, whose work usually forces them to spend time away from their kids. This was such a rare gift, something I've never forgotten or taken for granted.

My album was still in the charts when we went back to touring. Those first tours with Tal were real learning experiences. The good thing was that we were playing very kid-friendly rooms – lovely theatres, rather than smoky, dingy pubs, with decent backstage areas where I could set up a portacot for Tal – and we'd be done by 11 o'clock. It was all very grown-up. Tal would sometimes sit in his pram, quietly taking in the show from side-stage. Cori came out with us, too, which was a huge plus, and when he couldn't be there my Aunt Jenny would come and help out. Later on my cousin Sarah also helped out a lot on the road.

Cori was a hands-on father. We'd actually compete with each other to see who was first to change Tal's nappy, or to bath him and we rarely argued about parenting. We still don't. If there were autographs for me to sign after a show, and Cori was tired or busy, I'd grab Dad and say: 'Look after your grandson for a bit,' and everything would be fine. And, of course, the fact that I'd finish a show and race off stage to breastfeed my baby gave me plenty of material to share with the crowd each night. The one drawback was that the change in environment messed with

Tal's sleeping patterns – on a really bad night he'd wake as often as ten times.

Warners in the US were keen to get us back out there as there was the build from *The Sopranos*, and *Barricades*, which had been released there by then, was doing quite well. That meant they could get us good gigs and they could also book us on shows like Jay Leno and Conan O'Brien. So when Tal was eight months old, and Nash's boy Eden was two months old, we decided to head back Stateside for a big six-week-long trip, covering most of the country in the dead of the American winter.

Warners generously supplied us with two buses, because they knew that there was no way I'd tour if the children weren't properly catered for. The first bus was for the band and crew, which then included Dad, BJ, Jeff McCormack, Glen Hannah and Worm. That was the rock and roll bus, where the standard drink was beer. Then there was the nursery on wheels, with Mum, Cori, Veronica, Nash, the two babies, Talon and Eden, and me on board. On our bus the big drink was breast milk. I used to joke on stage that I wasn't sure which of our two buses smelled more strongly of vomit.

Frankly, I'd be happy to spend the rest of my life on a tour bus, with my family and the band next to me; it's an ideal way to live. These were very nice buses; Ozzy Osbourne had once used ours – yes, I checked it for syringes and headless bats; there weren't any. The rock and roll bus had the usual layout, with 12 bunks along the sides and a large room in the front and in the back. Ours had a large rear room with a double bed, which Cori, Tal and I claimed.

There were a few tricky thing about this tour; the weather for one. Because it was winter and snowing in most places it was a major operation to bundle up the babies and get them off the bus when we needed to. It also meant there weren't many opportunities to do those normal things that make up such a big part of any parent's day, and that I was keen to share with Tal: playing, going to the park, walking. We were pretty much bus-bound. And Tal, unfortunately, was going through a clingy stage, when he just wouldn't let me out of his sight. He would scream every time I left the bus to do promo, soundchecking and then playing the show. Once the gig ended, he was straight back on the breast and I'd settle in for another long night of frequent wake-ups and feeds. I got sick for a couple of days, so I was alternating between breastfeeding and vomiting, which did mix things up, but it wasn't quite the change I was hoping for.

It was at that stage that I grabbed Mum and asked: 'How exactly did you manage to take me out on the Nullarbor when I was three weeks old – *and not lose your mind*?'

Still, as difficult and challenging as this sounds – and it was one of the most demanding tours I've ever done – I tried not to lose sight of the fact that I was leading a charmed life. Most mothers with newborns would be chained to the house, dreaming of simply getting out to the shops, yet here I was, on the other side of the world, playing to enthusiastic audiences, surrounded by my family – and riding in Ozzy's old bus. Whenever I wanted to complain, a voice inside my head was saying, 'Suck it up, suck it up, this is every musician's dream' – and it was, though maybe not the baby vomit part.

I was also very fortunate with my American record company. Rick Gershon, who was my main person on the ground, was a genuinely decent man and a real music lover. He travelled with us quite often, and rarely came on the bus without a box of CDs, hand-picked selections for everyone in the group. I didn't always agree with Rick's taste – he was a massive You Am I fan, and I was still smarting from my own Tim Rogers run-in – but he loved music. He genuinely 'got' me – all of us. We all loved Rick, who we still catch up with when we can, and felt that he was on our side, if there were ever sides to be taken.

I think eventually Warners came to understand that as much as we loved touring in the US I wasn't going to move over there – I wanted to bring my kids up in Australia. They offered to set us up in a house in Austin, Texas, where we could write and live even part of the year, but it had no appeal; I lacked that burning desire to succeed there which would have meant relocating so we could build up a local presence.

What I did enjoy though were the audiences. In Australia, a lot of the time I was introducing people to the kinds of music I loved. In America there's already an audience for a certain type of country, blues, gospel and folk, for Emmylou Harris and John Prine. The audiences there got it, and I always felt that they were coming to hear the music rather than see me – I didn't have enough profile over there for that. But it was a double-edged sword – over there, I could easily have been just another person trying to make it on the alt-country circuit; in Australia, I had the field to myself for a long time.

We played some great gigs, at some beautiful and famous venues – we were getting our biggest audiences at this time. Of course I need to put that in perspective; while we were over there The Wiggles were also on a US tour. I ran into Murray from The Wiggles once when I was so excited about playing to an audience of a few hundred people at my own show. 'Where are you playing?' I asked him, only to learn that they were doing Madison Square Garden – for 12 sold-out nights.

I got a kick out of meeting other artists in the US; having Dwight Yoakam come backstage and introduce himself as a fan – and the rest of it. Benji Madden, from the pop-punk band Good Charlotte, came to one of our US shows and stood right down the front, a young guy with mad tattoos and the biggest Mohawk I'd ever seen, singing along to 'These Pines'; he was pretty hard to miss. We met him afterwards – this was before Good Charlotte became huge – and he was just the nicest guy.

Back home, as 2002 progressed, I'd occasionally be reminded of my success, but in the strangest ways. Cori and I were addicted to the game show *Wheel of Fortune*; we used to sit on the couch and play along as we watched. One day we were tuned in and 'Kasey Chambers/Not Pretty Enough' was an answer. Cori was too quick, and hit his pretend buzzer way before me. 'Oh my God,' I thought, 'maybe I am famous.'

But the reality of my life as a partner and mother would intrude quickly on these moments. At the ARIAS that year I got really lucky, winning Album of the Year, Best Country Album and Female Artist of the Year. The next day it was my turn to scrub the dirty jumpers for Cori's footy team.

But even when I won awards, my behind-the-scenes memories were always stronger than the awards themselves. My most vivid recollection of those ARIAs was something that happened at the after-party. Most of the booze, including beer, wine and some spirits, was free, but Worm was very insistent that we should have a round of shots, which someone would have to pay for. The way he saw it, I was the big winner and we should celebrate in style.

'Kase, give me some money,' Worm said, as he headed to the bar.

I'd dressed up for the night and wasn't carrying a handbag, and didn't have any cash, so Worm turned to Tony Harlow, who was there with us.

'Tony,' Worm said, 'I need some money.'

Fortunately, Tony loved Worm as much as I did, so he opened his wallet. He had a ten-dollar bill, a 20 and a hundred. Worm grabbed the hundred. 'This'll do,' he said. 'I'll keep the change. Just take it out of Kasey's royalties, okay?' And off he went to the bar. Tony smiled and shrugged. What could he say?

Worm, the champ that he is, usually helped carry my many bags when we were on the road, because he travelled light – and, well, I didn't. (You'd think after all those years living in a car I'd master the art of packing, but no.) Worm offered to help me as we neared the security check in one Oz airport, without knowing that Beccy Cole had planted a little surprise in my make-up case. The security guy was an Indian who spoke very broken English. He opened the bag and asked Worm whether it was his.

'Yes,' said Worm, happy, as always, to take responsibility for my stuff.

'Hmm,' said the security guy, who then pulled a vibrator out of the bag Worm was carrying. Not really sure what it was, he held it above his head, waving it around.

'What is this? What is this?'

'I don't know!' Worm replied, freaking out, backing away in horror.

Finally the guy worked out what he was holding in his hand, and shoved it back in my bag and told Worm to move along, quickly. And how did Beccy come to have this little surprise in the first place? From what I understand it was part of a 'buy one, get one free' deal.

It wasn't long after Tal was born that I was invited onto the *Rove* show for the first time. We went down to Melbourne, Cori, Tal and I, and were put up in the Como, a swanky, upscale hotel, miles from the sorts of cheap motels I was used to sharing with Worm while on tour.

After the show we went back to our room and fell asleep. Tal was in a bassinet next to the bed. I was feeling pretty good about myself – my record had done really well, I'd been on this popular TV show, we were in a nice hotel, life was good. In a little while Tal woke up and I checked him and realised that he was wet. So I brought him over to the bed to change his nappy, placing him on the beautiful white sheets. Just as I took off Tal's nappy, he did a massive poo, spraying crap everywhere. I stood there, thinking: 'Oh fuck, what a way to bring me back to earth.' Not really knowing what to do, I bundled up the shitty sheets and chucked them in the bin. I didn't get a bill, so I guess I got away with it. Kids really are the best reminders of the needs of the real world.

Tal was about 18 months old when a couple of big changes hit my world. I was starting to write some songs for the record that would become *Wayward Angel*, in between touring. One day when I was in Avoca, Tony Harlow called me out of the blue, saying that he was on his way back to Sydney from Newcastle.

'Can I drop in? I want to talk about something,' he said.

It wasn't normal for Tony to swing by unannounced. 'Of course,' I said, and spent the next hour or so wondering what he wanted to discuss while I prepared for the barbecue we were hosting that day.

When Tony arrived, Nash and I were in the kitchen with everyone else outside. Tony didn't say anything – he just looked at us and burst into tears. I got such a shock I began crying too. 'Oh my God,' I sobbed, 'is everything alright?' He regained his composure and said, 'I'm moving back to London. I'm leaving EMI.'

Amazingly, he was worried that he was deserting us by going home, which wasn't the case at all. Just the opposite; he had taken such a chance on me – and really on so many other young artists – and he had put work into making us a success in a way we felt comfortable with. I feel I was really lucky to have had such a good experience with my first record label; having talked to others, I know now how unusual it is.

I would miss Tony terribly but I knew that somehow he'd stay involved with our lives, we were that strongly connected, which proved to be true. I also understood that a good man was taking his place, John O'Donnell, a former journalist, label guy and another serious music lover. We'd be okay.

The other change started off much better, but it ended much more badly. While in WA on tour, Cori and I had a heart to heart about another baby. We agreed that we were ready, physically and emotionally, for number two and we had only great memories from my pregnancy with Tal and his birth. Things felt as normal as they would ever be.

Two weeks after Cori and I returned from WA, I fell pregnant. Again, we were completely over the moon. Straight away we let our families know, but no one else. The reason was not so much out of wariness about what could happen with the baby in those first 12 weeks, it was more about trying to not let it get out publicly. I was working towards the next album and I didn't want the distraction of everyone knowing.

I was struggling with the song that would become the title track of *Wayward Angel*. I wanted to express how I would be

Talon's wayward angel, on my own path but always there for him. I thought it'd be easy writing about being a parent, because it's such a powerful, emotional time, but it was almost too big for me to deal with in a song. It took more than a year to finish. It was the first song I started for the record, and the last that we completed.

About three months into my pregnancy, we were at home. I'd been really, really sick with the flu, which had been doing the rounds of the family. I was throwing up, violently ill, feeling horrible. A strange thing has stuck in my head about this one particular night: we were having lamb shanks, my signature dish, for dinner, although my appetite wasn't huge. Chris O'Hearn, from EMI, was coming for dinner, and just before Chris arrived, I'd had a little bleeding. I wasn't overly concerned. I'd had that while I was pregnant with Tal, and an ultrasound had confirmed everything was fine then. But the bleeding continued throughout the evening, and Cori and I made an appointment to see our doctor the next day.

At the appointment, my doctor asked if I'd been feeling any pain. I hadn't. He thought it best that I have an ultrasound. Up until that point I thought everything would be fine, but at the very moment they began the ultrasound, I knew something was wrong. I just sensed it. We could see the image of our baby on the screen, but it was like looking at a still picture, not a moving image. Cori and I looked at each other. The nurse didn't say anything; she left the room to find someone more senior to break the news to us. But we already knew the outcome. Our baby was gone. It was horrible. Horrible.

I clung to this faint ray of hope that maybe there was a problem with the machine, but that wasn't the case. The nurse who came back into the room said that our baby's heart wasn't beating. The baby had most likely stopped growing at around eight weeks.

We were gutted, absolutely devastated. We were now 12 weeks into the pregnancy and very emotionally attached to the baby; we had been preparing to break the news to everyone outside our immediate family. We'd actually said just that only days before: 'I can't wait until it's Monday and we can tell everyone we're pregnant.' I've got a big mouth; I was excited. What made it even worse was that I was in the same place where I'd been for all my pregnancy check-ups with Tal. Then, the place was full of life and excitement. Now, it was the complete opposite.

Straight away they checked me into hospital for a curette. Cori had come to the hospital with me, but wasn't allowed into the theatre so he sat outside while I lay alone on the table crying my eyes out, waiting to be put under. Then a nurse walked over to me. My face was puffy, my eyes were bloodshot, she could see that I was in very bad emotional shape, but she looked at me and said: 'Can I have your autograph?' I'm pretty sure she read through my look, which basically said: 'Are you fucking kidding?'

Once we left the hospital, Cori and I headed to Nash's house. What else could we do? Shane was there – he was working with Nash – and Worm was there, too. Nash and Worm knew what had happened, but I couldn't tell Mum, who was in Fiji. She called to see how I was but I decided not to spoil her trip with the bad news so I lied and said everything was fine. It could wait until she got back.

It was a very strange, detached evening. Cori and I should have been talking about what we'd just gone through, but instead we were almost too numb to talk at all; we sat around, played some cards and got drunk. I'd stopped smoking while I was pregnant with Tal, 18 months earlier, but I started smoking again that night, as did Cori.

I don't think I can articulate what was going on in my head apart from saying that I felt completely alone. Up till then Cori and I had shared a dream relationship, full of wonderful moments and life-changing experiences – including bringing our beautiful boy, Tal, into the world. But now, we seemed separated by something which should rightly have brought us closer together.

As I've tended to do over the years, I wrote a song about the experience, called 'For Sale'. That song is in part about the struggle I was starting to feel between my professional and personal life, but it was triggered by my miscarriage in particular. The first interview I did for *Wayward Angel* when it came out was with Bernard Zuel from *The Sydney Morning Herald*, where he asked me about that song and its meaning. I've always had a good relationship with the press, so, maybe in my naïveté, I told Bernard that I'd be totally honest with him, and I was, even though I wasn't overly comfortable with the possibility that my story would end up in print. I didn't mutter the words 'off the record' or ask that he not run with the story about my miscarriage, but when the article appeared, he talked about the larger meaning of the song and not my loss. I certainly admired the fact he didn't turn my misfortune into a story.

Cori and I actually did sit down and write a song in honour of our lost baby. It was one verse long; it was never recorded and I've never sung it live. Some songs are too private to share. It was also probably the only mutual grieving that I allowed us to do.

With Tal, things had gone from strength to strength; now they seemed to get worse and worse. Cori and I went back to the doctor and I asked how long it would be before we could try to get pregnant again. The doctor said that any time, medically, was okay, but psychologically and emotionally we should first deal with what had happened. Cori agreed with this, and tried reasoning with me, telling me I wasn't in the right place emotionally yet. But I had become obsessed with having another baby. 'I am fucking ready!' I would shout.

Now I know that trying to get pregnant again, straight away, was the worst way to recover from our loss. Then, I just desperately wanted to replace that life I'd lost. I was so one-eyed about it, I ignored the obvious – two people had lost something and both of us were in pain. I took it for granted that Cori was hurting too, but I felt I'd had the bigger loss. Knowing that many other women had been through the same thing didn't help me at all; I took it all deeply personally.

Mum came home from Fiji. I told her what had happened and we had a big cry together. We didn't tell Talon about the loss, he was too small to understand, but he sensed something. While I was pregnant, Tal would lie down with me and kiss my belly, and say something cute like 'Bubba'. He'd do it naturally, without any urging on our part. But he never did it after the baby went away.

In retrospect, something else died the night I lost our baby. Over the next year, as I withdrew into myself the way I do when I really feel confused, Cori and I drifted further and further apart. We just couldn't comfort each other. I tell myself that if our relationship had been meant to last, it would have survived this loss, but that is being wise in hindsight. At the time, there was no wisdom to be had.

I put all my focus into getting physically fit and well, thinking that if I got my body into shape, the next pregnancy would be okay. I joined a gym and my whole life began to revolve around the gym and my new fitness regimen. I was playing tough, pretending to be in control of my emotions, and making myself really unhappy in the process.

The attempts at pregnancy led nowhere. That was fortunate in a way because with things falling apart, we were in no state to become parents. Cori wanted our relationship to work out because there was Tal, and he tried harder than I did to make it work, but there came a point where it was obvious that Tal would be better off living in two happy homes rather than the one unhappy one he was in.

13

Starting over

If my heart turns blue
Would it still belong to you?

Lyrics from 'Bluebird'

One of the worst things about my break-up with Cori was that
for a while I lost a really good friend. He and I had been as much
mates as lovers, because we always had such similar personalities
and fitted so well with each other's lives. I was relieved when, in
the months after the final break-up, we started to regain that part
of the relationship and recall that, whatever had happened, we
really liked each other.

First, though, we had to live through a fairly public split. Up till
then I'd largely been able to keep the two parts of my life separate.
As a singer with a public profile I did get to walk the occasional
red carpet or do magazine interviews, mostly when I had a record
to promote. I had always known beforehand if I was going to be
in the papers, because I'd done an interview. That's the 'Kasey
Chambers' part; the rest of the time I'm at home writing songs,
being a mother and living a fairly normal life. So now when I

was in the news because of my relationship breakdown, I really couldn't believe that anyone else would care. But there it was, in the gossip columns. Most of what was said wasn't true, and some of it was so ridiculous that we even got a laugh out of it, but all of it was strange.

I think I probably got off lightly given what some public figures go through. But there were clearly downsides to my new success: the nurse asking for my autograph at the hospital, media offering money for shots of me and Cori and Tal; my life was no longer just my own.

Wayward Angel itself remains an album I am proud of, and despite all the terrible things which were going on around it there were lots of good memories from this time too. Co-writing with Cori, expressing some of what I felt about becoming a mother and especially getting to play with Steuart Smith who we flew over from the US and who brought such great tone to this album with his guitar.

Steuart is a legend in music circles and gracious to boot; when he wandered down to the local music shop once to get some strings for his guitar the salesman asked if he did a lot of guitar playing. Steuart said he did. Had he ever played in a band, the guy wanted to know. Yes, he had and still did. What's their name, maybe I've heard of them said the salesman. 'Well, they're called The Eagles,' said a bemused Steuart.

In September 2003, a great Australian passed away. Slim Dusty had been sick with cancer for a long time and a few days before he died I had a call from Chris O'Hearn from EMI warning me that Slim didn't have much time to live.

After he passed away, Joy McKean, Slim's wife, asked if I would sing at the state funeral. Normally I have an iron-clad rule about this; I get very emotional at funerals and so whenever I've been asked previously, or since, I just say no. But this was different; Slim was such a mighty man and had been such a help to all of us along the way, plus there was no way I could say no to Joy. And it wouldn't just be me singing with thousands of people watching in a church – Troy Cassar-Daley would also sing. We did a duet of Slim's 'Walk a Country Mile' and I managed to get through it without breaking down. Singing that song with Slim's family all looking on was terrifying of course – but it was such an honour too.

Wayward Angel did well on release, going to number one. With the album rolling along it was time for the annual trip to the US. Shane Nicholson, who had been working with Nash, was set to open for me on the tour. Shane had had some success with his band Pretty Violet Stain in Brisbane – they had been a Triple J Unearthed band and had gone to the UK where they signed a massive record deal, but then, as with so many artists starting out, it didn't work out according to plan.

Shane is not shy but he's completely unassuming and – the opposite of me – he only talks if he has something to say. I knew he was a brilliant musician, a beautiful singer and songwriter, who

I was really pleased was going to be opening for us, but I didn't know that much else.

A few days before we were due to go, I hosted a party at a house I'd rented in Copacabana, which was where I was living since the split with Cori. At some point everyone else had flaked out, except for Shane and me. I was feeling vulnerable and a bit drunk, and we had this little kiss. It was a bit awkward; I just thought, 'That was weird.' I'd never looked at Shane romantically, not even in a speculative way. When we met, I'd been happy and pregnant, he hadn't even been on my radar.

I didn't feel ready for a new relationship by any means. I was still heart-broken about the split, and about Tal who was being passed back and forth between Cori's and my house. And I had a tour to think about as well. A few days later – it was late November 2004 – we all left for America. Tal had come along on other tours but he would stay with Cori for that trip. I was worried about the strong feeling between me and Shane which had grown beyond a drunken kiss to something almost immediately intense. I thought, 'Why can't this happen in a year's time?'

The American trip was good for both of us, in a way, because we were a long way from our normal, everyday lives. It allowed us to enjoy our spark for a little bit without thinking too much about the complications waiting for us back home. Shane had come out of a six-year relationship a few months back himself, so both of us were carrying a lot of emotional baggage.

Shane and I had a few conversations about this during the tour, telling each other that it was probably best to resist what our hearts were telling us. But that'd last a day, at best. Still, I didn't quite get the chance to feel how I really wanted to. I almost felt bad, which seems crazy. It took some of the shine off that wonderful time when you first fall for someone. But it was all just so unexpected. Obviously Shane and I had a musical connection, but I don't think that was the starting point for us. I definitely needed someone, but I didn't want someone.

As usual, I was rooming with Worm while we were on the road. But there was one night, in San Francisco, where we'd headlined the Fillmore, when Worm was off with some friends, so Shane and I went out for dinner and some drinks, and then hung out at the hotel and watched a movie together. The atmosphere was slightly tense and full of unsaid things. Finally, I looked at Shane:

'You know that I'm in love with you, don't you?'

'Yeah, I know,' he said, looking straight back at me. 'I'm in love with you, too.'

And that was it. Now it was out there.

Shane and I made a mutual decision to spend some time apart when we were back in Australia. Shane headed back to Brisbane, but not for long. After one month we were back together, this time for good. That sounds very fast – which it was in a way – but we'd known each other for so long that it wasn't like going through the 'getting to know you' period of other new relationships. Musically, we had a strong bond.

But I was still sorting things out with Cori. I think we reached a point where we could see that there was a lot more good than bad in the relationship and it was worth saving the good. We had a great friendship. And he was a terrific dad. Neither of us wanted Tal to suffer for our mistakes.

We agreed to share Tal, but not in a legal, custodial way, a road we decided to never go down. Tal should spend an equal amount of time with both of us, which he does, and which has worked out better than I could have predicted. Tal, I'm glad to see, feels he got the best of the bargain: he's got two strong families who spoil him with love and affection, Shane's and mine and Cori and Danielle's, the woman he'd eventually marry, and someone who's become another member of our extended family. And of course someone very special to Tal.

A little while into Shane's and my relationship, I really wanted to meet his parents. I felt we were now getting too serious for me not to know his family. I'd actually met Paula, his mum, once, after a gig, when I was signing autographs, before Shane and I became a couple. She'd waved and mouthed, 'I'm Shane's mum – hi.' But she was gone by the time I finished up.

My family were part of our lives the way they always were – Mum lived down the road; Dad, his son Jake and Dad's partner, Kate, lived not too far away; Worm lived nearby with his wife, Bernadette. Nash, his wife, Veronica, and their boy, Eden, also lived close by. But Shane was from Queensland and his folks lived up there, in Redcliffe.

We arranged to spend a weekend with Ray and Paula, Shane's mum and dad, staying in their place where Shane had been raised. I am normally good at meeting people, all sorts of people; it's part of my job but it's also something I enjoy. But on this trip I had a terrible attack of nerves. I have no idea why, maybe I knew that Shane and I were heading somewhere serious and that if I didn't get on with his parents, that would be horrendous.

I spent the whole weekend edgy and uncomfortable and almost unable to speak. Me! People say I talk too much and it's true – Shane says one of the things that was attractive to him was that he didn't need to talk around me because I could fill up any silence all by myself. (Now, in the glow of married life, he also says he wishes I could occasionally be quiet.) But all weekend, I sat there trying to think of things to say. I hadn't taken Tal up with me that time so there were a lot of awkward silences.

On the Sunday afternoon when they drove us to the airport, I hugged them goodbye and, feeling they needed an explanation, I said, 'Look, I'm so happy to meet you guys, but I'm sorry, I was just really nervous this weekend.' Their response was, 'You have no idea how nervous we were about meeting you!'

It didn't ruin things, fortunately. A while later Shane and I were having dinner in the house at Copacabana where we now lived. An Emmylou Harris CD was playing; she was singing, 'It's gonna be easy, it's gonna be easy from now on' in the background, which captured our mood pretty well. But all evening Shane had been

211

behaving strangely, nervously, which wasn't like him. Suddenly he asked a question.

'Will you marry me?' he blurted out. Shane held out an engagement ring, which he'd had designed and made by my cousin Traci, who'd been out with me on the Nullarbor all those years ago.

I said 'Yes' without a moment's hesitation. We'd talked about marriage but it was still a wonderful, glorious surprise. It was perfect.

I wanted our wedding to be a special occasion, but when Shane and I talked about it, we also agreed that a traditional 'do' was not our thing. I had no desire to wear a big white gown for one thing. We thought about going somewhere exotic to get married, maybe on a beach, with all our families there. But we were shocked when we worked out how much even the smallest wedding would cost. To our estimate, the starting price was around $10,000. I'd made some money from record sales but it still struck us as an indulgence.

Then we had a better idea. Beccy Cole and I had been visiting children's hospitals and Ronald McDonald houses, usually around Christmas-time. We didn't do any media; it was all under the radar. We'd go in and play some Christmas songs for the kids, which was always a great but highly emotional thing to do, more so since Beccy and I had become parents.

At the Ronald McDonald house in Newcastle, I'd met one kid who really stayed in my heart. Jai was a cancer patient, one of five kids in the family, terribly sick at the time but with a smile that could light up a room. I met his whole family, who were staying there as well. His mum was lovely, as was his stepdad – and that struck a chord with me, because it was a reflection of Shane and Tal's relationship. Another reason why this sweet little boy stood out for me was that he had a little Spiderman T-shirt on the day that we met and Tal just loves Spiderman.

Both Shane and I felt strange about spending all this money on one day when we knew there were people like this family, doing it really hard, who could use some help. So we decided to give them the $10,000 we were going to spend on the wedding, and host a barbecue instead. It made the occasion special in a way that meant something to us.

We didn't tell most of the people that we invited to the barbecue celebrating our engagement in December 2005 that they were actually coming to our wedding as well. I had to let Nash in on the secret because he controls the purse strings and I needed money to pay for the celebrant and for chops for 30 people. The only other people that we'd let in on our secret were Aaron Laing, a good friend, whose company, Laing Entertainment, had booked our gigs for years, and his wife, Karen, who worked with Nash and helped us find a celebrant. But I didn't even tell Worm or Bern – Bernadette, Worm's wife and my closest girlfriend. I had my mind set on Worm being my Mate of Honour (I was Best Man at his wedding) and that was something I wanted to spring on him without any notice.

It was getting close to Christmas, a time of year when I really go overboard with decorations, so our house was done up in full Christmas style – fake snow, lights all over the place like the Griswalds' house in the *Vacation* movies. We had set up a barbecue on the balcony, and that's where our families and friends gathered. Shane's parents were there, along with his sister, Katy, and Steven, his brother. Mum and Dad were there, along with Dad's partner, Kate, as well as Nash and Veronica. Shane invited Bill and Edrie Cullen, his managers. Alex Lloyd, my labelmate and a long-time friend of Shane's, came with his partner, Amelia, and their little boy, also named Jake like Dad's boy. Of course all our various children were there.

You couldn't have guessed what was going to happen from the way we were dressed; I wore jeans, no shoes, and a Bob Dylan tour T-shirt and Shane wore jeans and a white shirt. As we all got settled, Nash stood up to make a toast. He thanked everyone for coming, and then said with his usual directness:

'Shane and Kasey agree that you are the most special people in their lives and they've decided to get married right here and now. Here's the celebrant, Sarah.'

Both our mothers, of course, burst into tears – tears of joy I should add! Everyone was stunned, and even Mum hadn't guessed. We handed a guitar to Dad and asked him to sing us a wedding song, James Taylor's 'You Can Close Your Eyes', which he used to sing to Nash and me when we were younger. It's not really a wedding song – but then again, this wasn't your typical wedding.

Worm, my Mate of Honour, did his bit in shorts and a T-shirt, no shoes, like the drunken uncle you see at family weddings. Brendan Fletcher, who made my 'Pony' video, and another long-time friend of Shane's, was there, too, taking the photos. And they're beautiful, all lovely, candid snapshots, even the ones of Worm, with a beer in one hand and a ciggie in the other and a huge grin on his face.

Our guests were shocked, but also really, really happy for us. Mum said that she was surprised she didn't pick up on it, because she knew I'd never go for the big wedding. 'I just didn't see the signs,' she admitted.

I had made all the food for the day. I have a real love of cooking and baking and I'd even baked my own wedding cake – two, actually. Since then I've been hired to make cakes for two other weddings, so I must have done something right. Food also turned up in my vows: I promised to make slow-roasted, red wine lamb shanks – my specialty dish – whenever Shane wanted. There's always a bowl of them in the freezer in case there's ever an emergency and I'm in danger of breaking my vows.

In the end, Shane and I did the island trip, but as a honeymoon, purely for ourselves, a few months later. We went to Vanuatu, so I guess we did indulge ourselves a little after all.

Under my contract with EMI I had a deal for four records. As we settled into our new married life, I started to think about my next record, which would be the fourth and final album with the label. I was really ready for a change of pace; all of my albums had been so autobiographical up till then, and I wanted to move away from that.

One of the more positive aspects from this time was that while Tony Harlow may have returned to the UK, one of our 'true believers' from EMI, Melita Hodge, left the company to work directly with us. That was one of the best decisions we'd ever made. She was the perfect foil to Nash as a co-manager; they got along brilliantly, never clashed, and Melita filled all those spots that Nash didn't.

Melita would come with me on video shoots and photo shoots, stuff that Nash didn't want to be involved with. Melita also became one of my best friends in the process. I couldn't think of another person that I clicked with on a professional and personal level quite like Melita. We were always on the same wavelength – if she thought something didn't look great on me, well, she was right. If I needed a dress for the ARIAs, I'd go to Melita. I still do, in fact, even though we don't work together officially any more. She's very honest; she has a great way of being straight without offending anyone.

I didn't want the songs on my new album to be about my marriage break-up, or about Shane. For once the idea of pouring my heart out to a bunch of strangers was completely unappealing, although I did manage to sneak in a love song to Shane, called 'Sign on the Door'. On another level, I also wanted to have some fun, to show my more girly side. As a younger artist I had wanted to prove I was serious, a serious singer-songwriter, now I was ready to show I could be playful as well. I wanted to make a pop album.

So everything about *Carnival*, as the album would be titled, was different. There was no acoustic guitar on it – and my whole career up to then had been based on acoustic guitar. I even took a new approach to writing. Normally I let the songs come out in their own time, and that can take days or even months. I'll put scraps of lyrics together, sometimes things that don't make sense, just to give a shape to the melody. Sometimes the stuff that doesn't make sense stays in – other times it comes out and is replaced by more direct lyrics. There's no one way. But this time I treated it like a regular nine-to-five job. Mum was away while I was writing and I went to her house every day and forced myself to write all day.

It was almost like a challenge album. I wasn't as connected personally to the songs like before, and I pushed myself to write about new things. Every other record has been my therapy: 'How am I feeling? What has been going on in my life? Let's write it in a song.' But this was different. And let's face it, no one's life is so interesting that you can write album after album about yourself forever.

I also got more involved in the styling, the cover, the artwork, more than I have ever done before. For most of my cover shots I'd been gazing off in the distance, but this time, I wanted to look really strong and confident and I knew I'd be looking directly into the camera.

There were a lot of new people playing with me, using different instruments – the drummer Michael Barker, Jim Moginie from Midnight Oil played guitars and lots of keys. Pete Dyball, a tech who'd come to play an increasingly large role in our touring world, helped out in the studio. And this was the first time I got to record with Tim Rogers from You Am I, with whom I'd later make my disastrous YouTube debut. There's a song on *Carnival* called 'I Got You Now', which I needed a male voice for. I tried to describe the particular voice I was after to Shane:

'It's not always perfectly in tune, but it sounds pretty cool, full of character,' I said.

'That's Tim Rogers,' said Shane.

He was right. Tim's voice fits in and his personality, which is crazy, fast, endearing, suits the track as well.

Recording with Tim was one highlight of the album; another was working on the song 'Hard Road'. Originally I recorded it by myself, but we felt it was missing something. When Nash suggested adding another voice, Bernard Fanning from Powderfinger's name came up. I knew Bernard, though not very well; certainly not well enough to cold-call him about a duet. I was keen on the idea but I had read an interview with Bernard where he said that although he liked rootsy music, he didn't like Hank Williams. Not like Hank! That just didn't make sense to me.

Hoping there was some way around our 'Hank differences' I sent Bernard a text message, explaining the situation and offering him every possible way out, in case he didn't want to do it. I wrote that I understood totally if he wasn't into the idea. He told me to send him the track, which was the right response – then he could base his decision on the song, not my waffly text message.

Two days later he phoned. He'd never called me before, and I was a bit nervous.

'Hey, Bernard,' I said, all casual.

Straight away, without prompting, he said, 'I fucking love it. I would absolutely love to do it.'

Not long after, Bernard, a very pregnant Clare Bowditch and I performed together at the ARIAs, singing his song 'Watch Over Me', and that ranks pretty highly among my musical moments.

Carnival was an album I planned as a bit of fun – and I did have fun making it. I wanted the album to sound colourful, and I think I achieved that. It was all about colours; that was why I called it *Carnival*. I've always thoughts of carnivals in terms of colours: colourful, but a bit mysterious. I wanted some of that with the record; I wanted it to sound happy and chirpy but also have this mysterious undercurrent. So it is ironic that it's become a reminder of such a grim period of my life that I never revisit it in my shows.

On the surface you would have said things seemed bright and promising. Cori and I had become friends again and Tal and Shane had bonded together. With the new album working out, Shane and I began thinking about having a baby, ideally before the end of 2006.

I had taken up smoking again when Cori and I lost our baby and I was still smoking when I started making *Carnival*. Someone once told me that if you give up smoking before the age of 30, your body would eventually revert to its non-smoking form, but if you continued smoking too long after that, it would be damaged forever. Even if I wasn't sure it was true, it got inside my head. I was 29 at the time. And I definitely didn't want to be smoking during pregnancy.

I didn't like the idea of being a smoker, although I didn't hate smoking per se. The worst thing about smoking, for me, wasn't about the smell, or the look, or even the health risks – it was that something controlled me; in this case, cigarettes. That really bugged me and became one of my biggest motivations to give up. Control freak? Me? Perhaps.

It wasn't as easy to give up as I had hoped. I tried everything – hypnotherapy, patches, going cold turkey. Finally I decided to try Zyban tablets, a drug that apparently was first used, unsuccessfully, as an anti-depressant (under the name Wellbutrin). It turned out that one of the side-effects of the drug was that people didn't want to smoke when they took it and it's now used strictly for people who are trying to quit smoking. I'm not a drug-taking person, prescription or otherwise, so I'd asked my doctor about it – his thought was I should try everything else first. But when I'd run out of other options I started taking the tablets.

The course lasted about three months. One day, I was reading the packaging, and I noticed something strange: it said that one of the possible side-effects of Zyban was anorexia. I remarked on it to Bern, Worm's wife, who I was with at the time, but I didn't think much more about it.

There were a lot of things I didn't think much about, that I didn't really know how to think about. I was about to go on what had becoming a familiar ride – do the album, do the promo, do the tour, probably head to the US, do some more gigs there, come back, start on another album. It was what I did – right? It was better than a million other jobs, it was all I'd ever wanted, and it was going so well.

So why was I feeling so crappy about it all?

14

Hard road

It could have been the colour of a carnival
It could have been the light in the dark
It could have been the blaze of glory
That keeps us all from falling apart.

Lyrics from 'Colour of a Carnival'

I can't think now why it took me so long to acknowledge that something was badly wrong in my life. Not just one thing – which is possibly why I didn't put it all together – but a whole lot of things, which would gradually build up into something major.

The bad year, as I think of it, unfolded in different stages. First, during my 'quit smoking' period, came the wildly emotional stage. That in itself should have been a warning sign. Normally I am the calm one, the one who, when everyone around me gets stressed, is the person saying, 'Don't worry, it's all good.' I never really allowed myself to get overwhelmed – I didn't feel I could. I was the centre of a family business, and if I collapsed, the whole thing would collapse.

But now I was going through constant mood swings; close to exploding over small things, short tempered with everyone around me. I thought it might be the tablets, so I gave those up, but the moodiness continued. It wasn't just anxiety and short temper; though I have never been a jealous person I was now becoming weirdly jealous of Shane's time and attention. If he went out to work on his computer at night – something he'd always done – I'd convince myself he wanted to get away from me. That he hated me, that he was indifferent. I would carry on like this even though I couldn't bear to listen to myself. I can't imagine what it was like for poor Shane; it was the worst possible way to begin a marriage. If there was ever a stage when Shane could have said, 'That's it, I'm gone,' that was it.

For most of my so-called *Carnival* time I was a wreck. I managed to complete a few tours, pleased as always to be up on stage, but for the first time I felt that I was going through the motions. I told all the usual stories and came across as this cheerful woman, the person everyone felt that they knew, but inside I was falling apart. Besides my obvious weight loss, no one except for those close to me would have noticed the difference. I think I was a great bluffer. Maybe I should have been an actress, not a singer! Ha, ha. I simply lacked the energy for it all, and no wonder, because I was also in the middle of an eating disorder.

I'm ashamed to say it now, but I'd always thought of eating disorders as a sign of weakness. Yes, like any woman, particularly any woman who has to do photo shoots as part of her job, I kept an eye on my weight. I talk about food a lot with my friends – cooking, as I mentioned, is one of the ways I relax, and I have been known to get carried away by healthy eating fads. The reason I was able to keep my increasingly strange eating habits secret for a long time was that diets are a regular part of my life. But this time it had become more than a diet.

I'd go for a week at a time eating very little, or only eating according to whatever dietary trend I was into at the time. After that I'd congratulate myself, lighten up and eat a piece of chocolate. Then straight away I'd say, 'Well, I've fucked up now,' and I'd sit down and eat as much as I possibly could of everything that I forbade myself from eating. I would carry a calories book with me wherever I went. I'd constantly check everything in my book before I ate it, and I'd add up every calorie that I'd consumed during the day. If I ate a Tic-Tac, I'd record it.

There wasn't a moment for an entire year that I didn't think about food and my body in one way or another. I'd dream that I'd caved in and stuffed my face, and would wake up feeling terrible. The obsession consumed me entirely.

When I dropped from 55 to 44 kilos people started making comments about my weight. But I'd just laugh it off. 'It's not as if I'm throwing up after my meals,' I'd say. Then I began eating things that would force me to throw up – too much chocolate cake, too many sweets, all in one sitting. I told myself that was okay too, because it wasn't as if I was sticking my finger down my throat forcing myself to be sick.

During the *Carnival* promo time, I travelled down to Sydney for a dress fitting. Melita was with me and it came up in conversation with her that a few people had asked if something was wrong. I looked very slim on the cover of the album, but I was looking much worse by then. I was also lying to almost everyone about it, so I lied to Melita too, saying there was no problem. It was astonishing how sneaky and self-deluding I'd become.

Melita and I went to a designer's showroom in Sydney where I was due to try on a heap of new clothes. For the first time in my life – and I've had plenty of these fittings – I could only fit into the smallest sample sizes, the clothes models could wear. 'Well, great,' the designer said, 'we've got tons of stuff for you.' Some people might have been thrilled, but I felt like shit.

I was so uncomfortable with myself physically. I looked in the mirror and saw bulges that didn't exist. I convinced myself I needed to lose more weight, so I'd get up and jog every morning. My family and close friends asked me all the time if I wasn't getting too thin. More than once Mum sat me down and asked how I was going, whether I was handling everything okay. I'd never allow myself to say that sometimes it was a bit hard. I'd tell her, and myself, 'No way, I'm the luckiest person in the world. People would kill to be in my position.' I was not going to sound like the poor little princess whose glass slipper didn't fit any more. Not me, no way.

Mum offered to take Talon for a few days, telling me every mother needed a break. But I said no. It was the only part of my life that I felt good about at the time – even though having an eating disorder was hardly the best mothering I could do!

It's funny: I doubted myself as a partner, a daughter, a sister, an artist, a musician, all those things, but never as a mother. I was very conscious of keeping it together when I was with Tal. I'd tell myself that it wasn't allowed to affect me being a mother. In fact, I found more comfort in Tal than anyone else at the time. When Tal was in the room with me, I didn't obsess about food, and I felt okay. Truly, it was the only time I wasn't consumed by eating and weight loss. Maybe it's that maternal instinct. I have no other real explanation, except that children don't judge, and Tal definitely wasn't looking at me and passing judgment, at a time when I felt that everybody else was doing just that.

Mum and Shane would talk to each other about what was happening, as I later found out – but nobody could get through to me.

I thought I was very smart about hiding my problem. If I went to dinner with other people I'd eat a decent meal, so that my mum would say, 'Okay, she's eating; it must be the exercise that she's overdoing.' But for days after that big meal I would eat as little as I possibly could.

Mentally of course I was a mess. I felt guilty about almost everything; guilty that I was doing this to Shane; guilty that I was doing it while my career was going so well; and guilty that Tal had a mum with an eating disorder. I felt guilty that I'd been given this great opportunity and that I was wasting it. Guilty that if I stopped touring, which I really wanted to do, that Mum and Dad and Nash would have no income. And when Nash or Mum would suggest I take some time off as I had gone four albums without a break, I felt guilty about that too – here they were relying on me and I was letting them all down.

Guilt on its own would have been bad enough but right behind it was the conviction that I was a fraud. I had pulled the wool over people's eyes for ten years but now, I was sure, they were about to find out that I couldn't write songs or sing. All those people who came up to me for autographs or bought tickets to my concerts would know that I had cheated them. I was embarrassed by the very thought.

My self-loathing started to leak into my dealings with the music world. Music had, in some ways, led me to this crisis. I was proud of *Carnival*, but I didn't feel connected to it, and when I began to think about it, the last time I had felt connected to music was when I'd made *Wayward Angel*. Admittedly it was only one album back, but it felt like a whole lifetime ago.

What had so long been a pleasurable part in my life was now an endless chore; it had taken over, it was controlling me. I began to hate it.

I couldn't listen to music in the house, I couldn't think about writing a song; it made me furious to even consider it. I didn't care if I never wrote again. Nash, wanting to be helpful, would say to me, 'You're just not in songwriting mode, it'll come back in a couple of months,' and I would secretly be thinking that I didn't want it to come back. I wanted to hate it for a while.

At my lowest, I was in a motel room in Sydney, on my own, and ate pretty much everything in the hotel mini bar – and then threw the lot up. What a waste of over-priced beer nuts! I called Shane, in tears, but I couldn't say the exact words that I needed to say. So I hung up and then sent him a text that read: 'I've just thrown everything up.' That's the point where he realised it was very serious. He asked me how long I'd been doing this, and I found it hard to lie to him, even though I'd been sneaky before. I just couldn't sugarcoat it any more.

Shane was a rock-solid presence all through this time; it still amazes me that he stayed with me. He said at one point, 'You need some help before we go onto this next stage of our life together. We're not going to have a baby until you're better.' I knew he was right, logically, but I was no longer responding to logic. I exploded, completely blew my top, screaming blue murder. I had a full-blown anxiety attack and ended up in a foetal position on the kitchen floor, sobbing hysterically.

In the midst of other fights I'd often walk out of the house, and jog up the street to Captain Cook Lookout. There was access for the public there, but I'd sneak under the wire fence and scale down the cliff a little bit further and just sit there, baseball cap pulled down tight, sunglasses on, crying my eyes out. Shane didn't know about this. I told him I was going for a run, nothing more.

I hated myself, so I didn't believe that anyone else could love me. That was especially the case after a 'binge night', something else I hid from Shane. He'd tell me that he thought I was losing too much weight, but to my twisted mind, he was a guy, he didn't understand what I was going through. I dismissed Nash, who also sensed something was seriously up, in the same way.

I've seen a lot of shows on TV with people who are obese, and realised it was the same obsession: food ruled my life, just as it ruled theirs. My obsession revolved around starving myself and then eating and throwing up. But it wasn't really about food at all or about being thinner. I honestly think that if you are wearing supermodel's clothes, as I was, you're too fucking skinny. It was wholly about control; about what I felt I could and couldn't say no to. Tony Harlow had been right when he wrote me his nice letter back when I was becoming successful; it was really important to know when to quit.

Bern, who's a teacher, and a pretty aware person, would send me messages, saying that if I ever wanted to talk, she was right there for me. I'd tell her that I was fine, and then ride the bus to Erina Fair, my local shopping centre, a place I've been to hundreds of times, and get the sense that everyone was staring at me and whispering things. I've never felt uncomfortable about being recognised, although I've never thrived on it, but when little kids stop and say hello, it makes my day. But now I was convinced that everyone was looking at me – and not because I was 'famous', but because I was too skinny, too fat, too everything in between.

It finally came down to that day at home, which I described earlier in the book, where Nash asked me a straightforward business question and I burst into tears. With him and Mum encouraging me, I was able to own up that I had a problem, and that it was beyond my or anyone else's control. I needed medical help.

Mum took me to a doctor and explained that we both felt I was underweight. The doctor agreed, but after speaking with me, he was able to see that there was a bigger picture here as well. 'Physically, I don't have to rush you to hospital,' he said. 'But mentally you're in a really bad way.'

My GP referred me to a female psychologist, who turned out to be the very person I needed then. Among other helpful pieces of advice, she told me to start writing a lot of things down, when I was feeling both good and bad. Her direction was, 'Don't write thinking that you'll ever have to show it to another person, or even yourself. Just write.' It was very therapeutic, it allowed me to set things out for the first time. One of the things that I wrote repeatedly was the word 'guilt'.

In late August 2006, I wrote one particular note while I was travelling to play a show. Even now, I still find it hard to read back:

I can feel the food digesting inside me, but not in the normal way. It feels as though it's releasing poison into my whole body, not just my stomach. I can feel the poison creeping down my legs, my arms, even my fingers and toes, rising up to my throat. I have to get it out. I am on a plane flying to Perth for a tour. My album Carnival *is at number one on the pop charts, but that does not take away any of this pain that I am feeling. I feel bloated and puffy. I just had this huge struggle with myself about whether to eat the airline food. I gave in and here I am, wanting to turn back time and starve myself instead. I know airline food isn't that good generally but that has nothing to do with the struggle inside my head. This is about all food. It's as though I eat food and then it turns around and eats away at me. It poisons my body, and, obviously, my mind. I know the logic in my head – I know I am not fat – and I know food is not poisoning me, but that's how it feels. I can't turn that logic into reality. It's like I have two people inside me: my logical self and my 'real' self that 'feels'. Feels anxiety, paranoia, it overwhelms me. My skin is sensitive to touch, my skin feels anxious. Is that even possible?*

I just threw up in the toilet. I didn't have to make myself do it; just the thought of the food in my stomach was enough to make me vomit. Now I have the guilt to deal with, although the guilt of vomiting feels much better than the guilt of eating. My anxiety has definitely gone a little, although the sadness I feel is probably a bit stronger. Not exactly sure why, it just is. Just hate not feeling myself, I guess. I used to like myself. Not much to like now. The weird thing is that I'm totally aware of my problem, totally aware of how ridiculous I am being, but if I had one wish right now it would not be to make all these feelings go away and to be better – I would wish to be five kilos lighter.

I'd read and re-read that particular note a lot while I was recovering, to remind myself how low I could, and did, sink. I didn't show it to my psychologist; in fact, I didn't show it to anyone. This is the first time I've ever shared it.

The recovery didn't happen all at once, and in some ways it's an ongoing struggle even now. Just sitting with someone, confessing to the many clashing forces inside my head – most of which sounded so odd in the light of day – was a long, hard process. At first I sugarcoated a little, but I quickly realised that there was no point in not getting to the truth. I had to make the decision to get well. I made the appointments, I turned up for the sessions. I looked forward to them, sort of, although I was maybe a little nervous. I knew that I couldn't be clever, as I'd been when hiding the facts from everyone around me. This person would know if I was lying.

It was helpful, more helpful than I would have believed, to say things out loud to a stranger. It was a relief just to have someone who didn't know me or have any expectations of me. Shane, Mum, Nash, fans, industry people, whoever, all had preconceived ideas about who I was. To be able to say what I was thinking, in my own words, I needed to speak to someone who I wasn't trying to please.

I see myself as a strong, independent person. I think a lot of other people also see me like that. I've done things my way. I make my own music – it may not be the coolest music on the radio, but it's the music I love. And that's the truth, that's how I feel about being creative. But being creative and having a career are two different things. During the creative process, when I'm writing a song or I'm in the studio, I'm not easily swayed by others. What comes after that is my job and it's a job which supports and involves my whole family, so I feel I have to give it some attention. If someone at the record label is saying 'Do this interview', 'Here's this promo tour', I feel they have invested in me and it is hard to refuse.

When you're standing outside the industry those two things look like the same thing. But creativity is not a nine-to-five job. I don't want it to feel like one. The pressure of making it that had worn me out.

I took Nash's smart advice about stepping away from music for a while. Yet even when that time had passed, and I felt relatively normal again, I knew that I didn't want to slip back into that old familiar pattern of recording and touring. If the thought of making another solo album entered my head, I'd think, not for ten years – that was the period I gave myself to think about going back to it. There were also periods when I thought 'Never again'.

It was fortunate in some ways that *Carnival* was the last record in my contract with EMI; this meant that there was no one politely asking Nash about my next album. With everyone around me laying down the law, I didn't think ahead about what would come next. I was still doing bits and pieces for *Carnival*, but if my career was over after that, so be it.

One of the few musical connections I had at this time was with Dad. He would come around and play me things he liked – and I could listen without feeling like it was a trap. A few times, other mates would come around and we'd play some songs together, songs other people had written. Eventually there were a few of us having a bit of a jam around at my place. Then we decided to play a gig at the local pub, the Avoca Beach Hotel.

Worm came with me to see the publican.

'We've got this covers gig we want to play,' we said. 'Can we do it in your dining room?'

I didn't want to play the front bar; I wanted to play before listeners, not drinkers. Thankfully, the pub owner said yes.

The core members of the band were Shane, Dad and me, as well as Chris Haigh on bass, with a floating line-up that was pretty much dictated by who was free on a Thursday night and could make it to the pub. Our original plan was to become a Neil Young-inspired act, going by the name Harvest. We had some posters made up, and spread the word a little bit among friends, and we advertised it in the local paper, where my name was just listed along with everyone else's. Yet just before we were set to play our first gig, Dad got an email from a Melbourne band named Harvest, who were about to release a record. They'd heard about us – I still don't know how – and asked very nicely whether we'd consider changing our name. So we adopted a new name, Lost Dogs, from *Lost Dogs and Mixed Blessings*, a John Prine album that we all loved, and which we planned to do a couple of songs from. Plus it summed us up; we were sort of sloppy, sort of casual, sort of without direction, and like dogs we were happy to be ourselves. All I wanted to do was to feel connected to music again, something I'd lost over the past year or so. I needed to feel something real.

I may not have felt like I was in control before, but I was really taking charge now. I laid down all these 'rules' before the band first played, for no other reason than I thought it would be challenging and fun. First up, I said, 'We are not doing original songs.' We were a covers band, but not your typical covers band. And we wouldn't do the same set two weeks in a row. I've always been a stickler for set lists and being over-prepared for gigs – I'll know what I'm wearing, for instance, days in advance – but that just wasn't the case with the Lost Dogs. There wouldn't even be a set list.

Instead I decided we'd go song for song: I'd sing one, then Dad, then Shane, whatever. What I really loved was the idea of being part of a band, just like the days of the Dead Ringers, rather than this person known as Kasey Chambers, out front of some backing group. I was one of three now, and I loved that straight off.

Our first gig was in July 2006. Nearby, at the beach, waves crashed onto the shore; inside on the tiny pub stage a revolution was taking place.

'We don't do originals,' I said, firmly but nicely to our audience. 'Don't yell out for "Not Pretty Enough", we're not going to do it. If you've come to the pub to get rowdy with your mates, then you might be better off in the front bar. Okay?' (The new me was right into cutting through the crap.) 'Now that I've got that out of my system – what covers would you like to hear?'

And that was it – away we went.

It was like that at every gig. If we knew the song people called out, we'd play it. There might be around 120 people squeezed into the room and they shared our tastes. We played Hank Williams songs, pretty much anything from Lucinda Williams, Patty Griffin, Tom Waits, Ryan Adams, Creedence. And Neil Young, of course – we played 'Comes a Time', 'Human Highway', 'Out of the Blue' and loads of others. Dad played his favourite Bob Dylan songs.

Most nights we had lots of fuck-ups. Loads of them. We didn't really learn songs, all we had was a chart book for whatever muso was playing with us. We didn't even tell each other what we were going to play. The rule was that while, say, Shane was playing his song, I'd be thinking about what I was going to play. Totally on the fly. One song would end and someone might yell out: 'Powderfinger.' So we'd have a shot at 'These Days'. That's how most nights went.

As the weekly gigs continued, lots of musos heard about the show, and would turn up. They had to pay the $12 cover charge, unless they sat in with us. And some really great artists came to the gigs: Diesel, Troy Cassar-Daley, Sara Storer, Beccy Cole, Bec Willis and Sarah Humphries. We'd invite some up-and-comers to play a set, or even pull people out of the crowd to sing with us. Jeff McCormack would come along and play, as would James Gillard and fiddle player Mick Albeck, people we'd gotten to know really well over the years, which made the gigs feel homely and comfortable, totally relaxed. We settled into a sort of routine: the Lost Dogs would play a set, then the guest would play a set, and then we'd finish the night. Sometimes our guest would hang around and play that final set with us. Kevin Bennett, the leader of the great band The Flood, became such a regular that he was made an unofficial Lost Dog.

It was a bit like the days of the Dead Ringers when music was a way of having fun. The Lost Dogs helped me regain my love of music; they were as important as my sessions with the psychologist. We got a free pub meal – which I didn't throw up – and spent a couple of hours playing unrehearsed favourites with our pals, to a crowd that became our friends. That was reward enough.

We played almost every week for about a year, and pretty much filled the room each time. It was a motley crowd who came along: there was a small, hardcore group who'd drive up from Sydney; there were some 'Fred Heads' who couldn't get enough Fred Eaglesmith (Shane played a mean version of his 'Alcohol And Pills'). There was one guy who sat down front and videoed almost every Lost Dogs show. He was the ultimate bootlegger, bless him, who'd been a fan since the Dead Ringer days.

We'd play tribute shows: we hosted a Hank Williams night, a Woody Guthrie night, and on another week we played every Jimmie Rodgers song that we knew. We had themes, too, including a night where everyone had to dress in khaki, a tribute to the great Steve Irwin. And there were on-stage musical challenges: one week I sang Toni Basil's 'Mickey' and a crowd singalong began out of nowhere, totally unscripted. Another time Shane took on 'I'm Too Sexy'.

For Shane and me, the Lost Dogs were a way of growing back together after what had been a rocky start to our marriage. Both of us were coming off our most commercial-sounding records – *Carnival* for me and Shane's *Faith and Science* – and both of us wanted to do something different. Sitting next to Shane on Lost Dogs nights, playing my favourite covers – with him on electric and acoustic guitar, lap steel, banjo, mandolin and singing along in his beautiful voice – was one of the most rewarding musical lessons I've ever had. We grew back together through music.

We talked a lot about doing an album together – and we wrote a whole lot of songs which would eventually end up on our LP, *Rattlin' Bones*. When we didn't have a guest one week, I told the crowd: 'We're going to be the guests tonight and we'll play originals, for this one time only.' That night we played a few of our new songs for the first time. I played Shane's 'One More Year'.

I was having so much fun with the Lost Dogs that the only worry was whether I'd ever want to perform on my own again. I did of course have to do a few of my 'regular' gigs from time to time, festival spots and so on. But it was the Dogs taking centre stage. We even took the band on the road a couple of times, to Tamworth and the Bluesfest at Byron Bay. It was fun, but the Avoca Beach Hotel was our real home, a room with people we knew and could relate to in it. We knew the audience so well, we could share the big news of the time when it happened – I was pregnant again, finally.

15

The ballad of Barnesy's bin

I'm a wildflower by the highway
Up against the rain
I'm an old man, growing tired
Getting used to the pain.

Lyrics from 'Wildflower'

Arlo may have been born in the same Central Coast hospital as Tal, on 16 July 2007, but his birth was unlike Tal's in almost every way imaginable. For one thing, he ran way over time.

The week before he was born, Shane and I even went to see Vika and Linda Bull play at our favourite local venue, Lizotte's, in the hope something might happen. The way I figured, if there was one voice in the country so powerful that it might bring on my labour, it was Vika Bull's. But no luck. (Don't get me wrong, I would have checked out the Bull sisters if I was pregnant or not, I love what they do.)

For much of the two weeks leading up to my due date, Shane's parents, Ray and Paula, and his aunt Annie, had been down from Brisbane, staying with us, and helping out where they could. By the time they were booked to go home I was still very pregnant. Shane, who was feeling as exhausted and frustrated as me at the non-arrival of our first child, was ready to zoom me off to the hospital at the first sign of anything that even resembled labour. As for me, my back had been killing me during the final stages of my pregnancy. I'd been ducking out every few days for acupuncture, in the hope that it might ease the pain a little bit. I was a little over the whole pregnancy thing, tired of waddling around and feeling like a blimp.

'Come on, kid, where are you?' I asked my swollen stomach.

On July 14 we went to see my doctor who examined me and said that if nothing had happened by the following day, he'd check me in and induce the baby. I had this checklist of things that I didn't want to happen during pregnancy: I didn't want to be overdue; I didn't want to be induced; I didn't want to have a Caesarean; and I wanted to be able to breastfeed. I was still stubbornly holding out for all of those, little knowing that by the time Arlo was born, I'd be crossing most of these so-called essentials off my maternal wishlist.

My situation hadn't changed by the next morning, so I was checked into the hospital and induced. (So strike that one off my list, for starters.) Mum and Shane were with me; Tal was with Cori. Time dragged along, and the three of us nodded off to sleep. But about an hour after being induced, I woke up to go the toilet when – bang! – my water broke. I gave Shane and Mum a nudge. 'Okay, we're on,' I told them, and then pretty much went straight into serious labour. Within another hour I was in a lot of pain, a lot more pain than when I went into labour with Tal, although I may have just erased that from my memory.

I'm pregnant as I write this, and realise that I'd like to experience pre-labour with my next baby – it hasn't happened to date!

After my happy epidural encounter when giving birth to Tal, I'd become an advocate so I didn't think twice about asking for one this time around. But while it did ease the pain the labour just dragged along. I got to the stage of being nine centimetres dilated, which was about eight hours in, and then ten centimetres, but still nothing. My doctor, who had also delivered Tal, and would deliver Townes, Worm and Bern's baby, told me that if nothing happened within the next 20 minutes, it was C-section time. I cried and cried. I'd been through that much pain and now felt that I'd gone through the last nine hours for no reason.

'Let me keep going until it's the only option,' I sobbed, and the doctor reluctantly agreed.

Yet within 15 minutes, my baby's heart rate dropped. Basically, as I'd soon find out, he was just too big. It was now getting on for five in the morning and I was told that I couldn't wait any longer without putting the baby at risk.

'We're taking you down now,' the midwife said and this time there was no debate.

We'd gone from 'let's have a talk with Kasey and Shane about a C-section' to 'right, we're going downstairs', all in about 15 minutes. I was set to cross another essential off my pregnancy wishlist.

In the theatre, I spent the first ten minutes vomiting like a geyser, probably in reaction to the epidural. They put a sheet over me and started prep for the C-section while I threw up, though I was able to stop before the next stage began.

The doctor asked Shane if he wanted to see certain stages of the birth, and he told me how amazing it was to see me opened up, with our baby's face protruding from my stomach, looking up at him. A nurse took some incredible photos for us. Weird, amazing photos, which I might keep to myself. Luckily I couldn't see or feel what they were doing; the whole process would have been a bit too gruesome for me, I think.

At the last minute, just as our reluctant baby was finally emerging, I turned to Shane and said, 'I hope it's a boy.' Now, we'd never said that we would prefer one sex over the other, but he looked at me and said: 'Me, too.' Then I felt really bad. 'What if it's a girl?' What a terrible start that would be for any kid! Fortunately, it was a boy.

When they pulled Arlo out, I couldn't believe how big he was. He was absolutely massive – nine pounds ten ounces. No wonder he'd been having such a struggle. When I'd gone in for check-ups along the way, I had been told: 'Oh, it's a big baby', but I'd heard that with Tal, too, and he turned out to be average-sized. Not so with Arlo. He took a while to breathe, which is normal with C-section babies though I didn't know it at the time. Shane and I waited, a little fearfully. 'You can touch him,' the nurses told us. 'He's yours.' And then after what seemed an eternity, Arlo began to breathe.

I couldn't hold him at first, because my arms were numb from the drugs, so Shane gathered him up and placed him on me. I thought to myself, 'How can it be that the most beautiful thing in the world can resemble some kind of alien?' He and Tal looked nothing like each other when they were born. Both were odd-looking; all babies are, I guess. But I still couldn't get my head around his size. When they told me his exact weight, I had this little flash: 'Maybe I'm glad I had a C-section.' We'd picked out his name in honour of Arlo Guthrie, a singer who I really admired; Dad used to sing us loads of Arlo and Woody Guthrie songs. We took his middle name from Shane's Dad, Ray.

Tal had arrived at the hospital with Shane's parents by then. He didn't want to miss out on the sibling he'd been waiting so many months to see. He had already written a song for Arlo called 'I Love You So Much Even Though You're Not Out Yet'. When we'd told Tal about the pregnancy it had been Christmas and we told him the baby was his Christmas present, so he had asked could he be the first to hold the baby when it was born. I explained that Shane and I would probably hold him first, but he could be next, absolutely. I have a beautiful shot of Tal with Arlo in his arms in the theatre. He was just so chuffed.

The biggest surprise for me was Shane. He's not the most outwardly touchy-feely person; he's not a hugger! And that's fine – I don't need that 24 hours a day. A woman in labour has different needs, anyway. As a birthing partner, he was amazing; focused, telling me all the things I needed to hear. He touched my head at the right time, held my hand at the right time and lied when it was necessary – 'Yes, babe, the drugs are on their way.'

I feel that having a C-section, while it was unavoidable, did make this a very different kind of birth experience than for Tal. Obviously I feel just as connected with Arlo as I do Tal, there's no question of that, but having a Caesarean, as opposed to a natural birth, really did feel different: much more clinical, a bit artificial. I don't know why that is, it's hard to explain. I don't even know why that meant so much to me. And it wasn't a physical thing – a certain amount of pain comes with either type of birth. But I do know that with my upcoming baby, I'm going to try and opt for a natural birth.

I'd been preparing Shane for the absolute worst-case scenario when we came home.

'Sometimes,' I told him, 'they're up ten times a night, and you never get proper sleep.'

Then of course, Arlo was the absolute dream baby, who slept most of the time, ate when he needed to, and didn't create too much of a fuss. I was almost disappointed that Shane didn't get the full newborn experience.

From the start, Tal was incredibly protective of his little brother, possibly even a bit over-protective. If we ever get cranky at Arlo about something, Tal will pull us up and say: 'He's only little, he doesn't understand.' The five-year difference between them is not planned but it's worked out just perfectly. Tal is grown up enough to understand, and appreciate, his responsibilities as a big brother, but not so old that they can't hang out together.

I've enjoyed watching their relationship develop as much as I've loved my own ever-changing relationship with both of my boys. If it's the part of the week when Tal stays with Cori, he'll call us, but only to talk with Arlo. When Tal stays with us, all he wants to do is play with him. Even when Tal's friends are over, he insists that his little brother joins in, well, most of the time. Arlo responds to all this love, too. Now, when I ask Arlo what he wants to be when he grows up, he simply says: 'Tal.'

Not long after Arlo was born, I was lucky enough to welcome Tyler, another baby brother, into our lives. That made two little brothers, almost the same age as my little boys – I love it. The more the merrier, I say. And when Dad and Kate married, that meant I now had two stepsisters, Ashley and Hayley, who are also part of our big, crazy, ever-expanding family. Nash and Ronnie now have four children: Eden, Skye, Bela and Liam, so with my third on the way, the Chambers family keeps on growing.

For much of 2007, Shane and I had been writing new songs for what would become *Rattlin' Bones*. It was a complete departure for both of us in so many ways, more like a Lost Dogs record than a 'normal' LP. It wasn't autobiographical, most of the songs came out of imagery, Southern Gothic imagery, if you like. And of course it was the first time we'd seriously written anything together – though we'd talked about it on and off for ages.

I'd co-written with a few people – Cori had three co-writes on my *Wayward Angel* record, and Worm and I had written some pieces, too. Writing with Shane, however, was a little more intimidating. He's a true songwriter, a craftsman, someone who needs to write every day, whereas I only write when I feel the need to get something out. For him, it's his lifeblood, for me it's therapy.

I put it off for a long time. But Shane chipped away. 'Let's get started with that record. How about tonight?' he'd ask me while I was making another excuse or faking a headache. I worried that we might not have a creative spark. I knew that we could sing together, live together, travel together, be parents together – but what if we couldn't co-write a song?

It was a needless worry. Our first songwriting session took half a night and resulted in the song 'Rattlin' Bones'. It was a totally different type of song for me. It felt pure and genuine. I didn't think what it was about – later when people asked us, we'd generally make something up – it just sounded good to us. Sometimes that's all music is.

We had some songwriting sessions where nothing happened, but more often than not things fell magically into place. Occasionally we'd get halfway through a song and get cranky at each other and stop, but I'm still surprised at how well we got along creatively. I thought, wrongly, that when you put two creative people in a room together sparks could fly, but not always the good ones. That proved to not be the case with us.

Shane's really good at co-writing: he knows when to suggest something and when not to. He's very polite, and has a way of making me feel that everything I offer is worthwhile. It also helped that he's a multi-instrumentalist. I'd get halfway through a song and say, 'You know, a mandolin might sound good here.' Typically I'd file that away until we got to the studio, but Shane would say: 'Great, let's try it now.' Two minutes later he'd be sitting there with a mandolin, or whatever we felt the song needed. I'm not much of a guitar player, I tend to go for the same feels, the same chords, so working with Shane helped take songs in interesting, different, unexpected directions.

Our songwriting styles are so different, in much the same way that our personalities differ: I'm really vocal, I have to sing something over and over to get to the next line, whereas Shane sits and thinks about it for a while, and then comes up with a line. The extrovert and the introvert, basically. And our approach is different in other ways. Before working with Shane I'd usually finish a song in one sitting, then never touch it again. Shane is the opposite; as he says, Leonard Cohen is still rewriting 'Hallelujah' 30 years after he first sang it and if it's good enough for Leonard Cohen … He will often change his songs, change the lyrics, play them differently live than on a record.

The only song that we found ourselves stuck on was 'Wildflower'. Eventually this became a song written for Arlo, and we'd started it before he was born – about half the songs were done before Arlo was born, the other half soon after his birth – but we just couldn't find the right lyrics for this one piece of music. We tried and tried and just couldn't work it out. Then Arlo was born and the lyrics came pouring out; it was as if they fell from the sky. We figured, 'Well, there weren't any lyrics because Arlo hadn't been born yet. He wasn't here for us to write about him.' Weird yet kind of beautiful, too.

At that stage we weren't signed to any record label. Things were changing so much in the music industry that my old label, EMI, was now full of people I didn't know well. We made the decision to fund the record ourselves. With luck we'd sign up with the right company once it was finished; if not, we figured we could sell it at gigs ourselves.

It's funny how things happen. We were looking for a studio in which to make the album. Nash had been working with Jimmy Barnes, who has his own house-cum-studio in Botany, in the south of Sydney. Jimmy and his family would be overseas for Christmas 2007 and New Year and he offered us the use of his place.

By the time we got into Barnesy's studio, Shane and I had it pretty clear in our heads how all the songs should sound. All that baggage that comes with making a record, knowing that a major label was paying the bills, was no longer in play. It was an incredibly liberating feeling for us – and could there be some strange cosmic connection that we ended up signing with a label that was actually called Liberation?

We took what was almost a Lost Dogs approach to things – after all, this felt like a record that the Lost Dogs would make, if they ever got into a studio, so why not continue with that idea of messing with the formula? We agreed that the record would essentially be made live. Shane and I even sang our vocals looking at each other, and often we'd share the one microphone. It was very old-fashioned record making, in a way. Very country.

Because people knew Shane as being a pop/rock guy, I think they assumed I pulled him in a more country direction, over to my side of the musical fence. But that just wasn't true. Shane drove this album more so than me; I tagged along. We only had one major blue in the studio. It was during the song 'No One Hurts Up Here', which Dad, Shane, James Gillard and I all played and sang around one mic, 100% live.

I wanted to record it in one take, because I hate singing songs over and over again. Typically, I do three or four takes, Nash picks out the good and bad bits, and works it together. I told Shane, who was co-producing the record with Nash, 'I want to get the entire song, from start to finish, in one take.' But someone, often me, would mess it up each time, so Shane's suggestion was, 'Let's just piece together two takes.' I dug my heels in; we sang it a few more times but it didn't work. Doors were slammed, voices raised, and I said, 'That's it, I'm done for tonight.'

The funny thing is that when we made up later, we did get one really good take, and I said, 'See, it was worth it.' Shane smiled and said, 'Kase, you're not there in mixing and mastering. What ends up on the record, well, you won't really know, will you?'

One of the interesting things about *Rattlin' Bones* is that there's only one drum track on the entire album, played by John Watson – the rest of the percussion is Shane and Mark 'Bucky' Collins hitting pots and pans and other things we 'borrowed' from Barnesy's kitchen. Shane really wailed on this one particular tin garbage bin that we found, and hit it so many times that he wrecked the thing. When we left we took it with us, hoping Jimmy wouldn't notice it was gone. So we not only used his stuff, and his house, but we wrecked and stole things, too. Great guests!

That was another wonderful thing about making the record: we got to live in Barnesy's house. All our kids were there with us, while Mum stayed and cooked for everyone. It was the closest, warmest feel I've had since making *The Captain* out on Norfolk. *Rattlin' Bones* had that same sense of family, of closeness. It was a great, fun experience from beginning to end. And, once again Jimmy, I'm really sorry about the garbage bin.

One of the key influences for the record was the work of Kieran Kane and Kevin Welch, two of my favourite singer-songwriters. In fact we asked Kieran to be in the band for the album, but timing-wise it didn't work out. Next time I saw Kieran, he said that he was really disappointed that it didn't come together.

'I'd love to do a record with you guys,' he said, which was quite an accolade.

I laughed. 'It doesn't matter, because we pretty much stole all your ideas, anyway. But this way we didn't have to pay you.' Hopefully we'll work together one day.

The *Rattlin' Bones* record was done, but the Lost Dogs hadn't finished yet. I only missed one gig when Arlo was born and then I was back the next week, wincing a bit because of my C-section, but still full of enthusiasm for the band and the gig and the people.

Arlo's first gig, a week after he was born, was the Lost Dogs, and I'd bring him along to the shows from then on in. Mum would look after him backstage while I played. It was a real family affair; I was on stage with my husband and my dad, my new baby was nearby with my mum, and Tal would be there sometimes, too. Occasionally I'd break off mid-set to collect Arlo, find a quiet spot and breastfeed. No one seemed too concerned.

But with *Rattlin' Bones* about to come out and a solo tour on the schedule, there was a time when I couldn't guarantee turning up every Thursday night. On what became the final night of the Lost Dogs, 21 February 2008, we simply let people know that there'd be 'special guests', whereas usually we'd let them know in advance who was playing with us. I baked about 200 'going away' cookies for everyone, and handed them out during the break. Then Barnesy got up and played a great set, seven or eight songs, all country, everything from George Jones to Freddy Fender, Roy Orbison and more. It was a great night and a sweet farewell.

Just like the Dead Ringers, the Lost Dogs never really broke up. By the time I had to get back to my regular day job we were ready for a little break. I didn't want to get sick of it; I was fearful of running it into the ground. So now I keep the band up my sleeve for when I need to get back in touch with music again.

Meanwhile we were running around making videos, doing photo shoots and everything else we needed to do for the *Rattlin' Bones* record. As we agreed, we started thinking about labels once the work was almost done and we felt we had a record we were really happy with. Nash had met Warren Costello, who runs Liberation Records with Michael Gudinski, through working with Barnesy, and he told me that Warren was a very easy-going, music-loving guy, and that the label was doing some interesting things. 'Maybe we should talk with them,' Nash suggested.

I hadn't met Michael Gudinski before but you can't work in the music business without knowing something about him and from what I knew, I wasn't sure we would click. He is the man who has signed up hundreds of Australian acts from Skyhooks to Kylie Minogue while heading up Mushroom Records. To me, he seemed like a real music-biz type, fast, sharp, always looking for an angle, as far from Tony Harlow as you could get. I couldn't have been more wrong.

Warren is very quietly spoken, a level-headed person, a real gentleman. Michael is the opposite; wildly inspired, innovative, a guy who wants to do things other people haven't and doesn't care much what people think about him. At the first meeting my thought was 'Oh my God, he's such a full-on guy', but it was infectious – Michael is a big personality but he cares about music and that is what drives him. Our instincts told us to go with Liberation; they were smaller in a corporate sense to what we were used to but they had big, new ideas.

They're also the label for Bliss n Eso, a local hip-hop duo who once did some recording with Nash at his place, way before anybody had heard of them or us, and who we've gotten to know a little bit and record with.

No one from the label had heard *Rattlin' Bones* when we brought it to them, but they had no hesitation agreeing to our terms. In the end, at the time of *Rattlin' Bones* we changed everything – record label, booking agent and music publisher – and they're now all under the Mushroom/Liberation banner. That appealed to me, having everything in the one house, so to speak. I tried to sack Nash and get a new manager, but he wouldn't allow it. (Just kidding.)

Liberation pushed for radio but didn't get a huge response, which was no great surprise to Shane and me, it wasn't that kind of record. But it didn't seem to matter; the record just somehow resonated with people, becoming my fifth record in a row to go platinum in Australia, debuting at number one. And it was an album and a tour where some new rules came into play. I divided the creative side from the career side – promoting was my job and I could have fun with it but I kept it in my head that it was the business side of what I did. It didn't need to intrude into the other parts to my life – looking after my kids, being with my family, and I made sure I had enough time for that. I can't say I always manage to get the balance right, but I am learning.

It helps to have Nash as my go-between. He and I sit down to discuss all aspects of what I do, from where we might tour this year, to who will be the opening act, to what interviews I will take part in and when. He's the kind of business head I need; as he'll say, half joking, it's always got to be at least 51% about the music. He knows me so well that if something feels wrong, he will just say no.

We toured *Rattlin' Bones* consistently for about 18 months, including a few visits to America, where we had a new label, Sugarhill Records, who were pretty similar to Liberation in size and approach. Sugarhill is home to such acts as Guy Clark, Ricky Skaggs and – believe it or not – Robert Earl Keen.

16

One huge baby and seven little hillbillies

Dad, do you remember
When I was a little girl
Did I wonder where I came from?

Lyrics from 'Dad, Do You Remember?'

In May 2008, Dad went out to play at the Norfolk Island country music festival, where we'd had that chance encounter with the Menghetti family all those years earlier. All the artists at the festival were invited to the local school, to play for the kids there. On the way out, Dad realised, 'Shit, do I know any children's songs?' Then he thought about what kid-friendly songs he did know. One that stuck in his head was Taj Mahal's 'Annie's Lover' – hardly the name for a kids' song, come to think of it. But it has chicken noises, all these crazy animal sounds. It's a lot of fun, right out there.

When they got to the school, everyone else was playing Wiggles and Hi-5 songs, so when Dad played 'Annie's Lover', surprisingly enough it brought the house down. He used to do it at Lost Dogs shows, too, and the response was just as mad. On his drive back into town, Dad said to his wife, Kate: 'Maybe I should make an album of children-friendly songs, and get all the little kids in the family on it.' He soon came up with the name Poppa Bill and the Little Hillbillies. The original plan was an album of covers of his favourite songs from when he was a kid. But that would change when I got hold of the idea!

At around the same time I had been speaking to Bern, Worm's wife, about doing a kids' book. It had been a dream of mine for as long as I can remember; I even had the characters in my head ready to go. So when Dad came back to the coast and he mentioned the kids' record, something clicked. I hadn't written a song since 'Woe is Mine', the last song we wrote for *Rattlin' Bones*, but that night I sat down and wrote a few songs, including 'The Ballad of Poppa Bill' and 'I Spy'. It was a real burst. I was totally inspired – again, it was all about doing something totally new and different.

The plan, if there was one, was that these songs could appeal to children first and foremost, but musically speaking, and sometimes lyrically, too, they wouldn't have been out of place on my own 'proper' albums.

The next day I called Dad up and said, 'I've got three songs for the album.'

There was a silence on the line. He said, 'What album?'

'The kids' record,' I said. 'I'm onto it. Let's write some more songs.'

Dad said, 'You're taking this very seriously, aren't you?' And I was. I was really excited about it.

Dad was in the middle of recording a solo record, but he put that on hold and we started to get together and write. The first thing that we came up with was, 'Dad, Do You Remember?', one of my favourite songs on the record, a very personal thing. It was a real little moment for both of us, writing and recording it. It sounded like it would fit on one of my records, yet it was kiddie friendly – and adults could relate to it, too. It set up the record perfectly.

Then Worm and I got together and wrote 'Christmas Time' while Bern and I came up with 'Before You Came Along'. She'd never written a song before. It came to us one night at my place when we were sitting around having a few drinks. Bern and I had been writing the children's book together – she's a teacher and had a real feel for writing – and from that I could tell that she might have a spark for writing songs. We started talking about our lives as mothers, and what changed for us after we became parents, how the good outweighed the bad, that kind of thing. That's where 'Before You Came Along' came from. We'd planned for Worm to help out, too, but he passed out before we started writing.

The title of the book was *Little Kasey Chambers and the Lost Music* and we decided it would go with the record. Bern also came up with the idea of writing in verse, as I would in a song; she really got the project moving. If it was an album, she would have been the producer. And then the guys from Liberation also got totally behind it. Michael Gudinski has his critics, but when you work with him, you just need to suggest an idea he likes and he is away.

What's not to love about someone with that kind of spirit and drive?

I'd told Tal about the record, and one night he said: 'I want to write a song for the Little Hillbillies.'

'That's great,' I said. 'What's it going to be about?'

He often walks around the house making up songs; he's interested in songwriting, although I've never pushed him.

Tal asked me: 'Well, what do you write about?'

'My life,' I said, 'how I feel about things.'

So we agreed that he'd write a song about how he felt, something that made him feel special. Tal said, 'Well, I feel special because I have two houses. Some of the kids in my class only have one mum and dad.' He was the lucky one, in his eyes! Cori and I have never let him feel that there was a negative side to our arrangement. And because we all get along so well, he has no reason to feel negatively: he has two sets of parents, two houses, two rooms, two sets of toys. So that was the theme for his song, 'Two Houses'.

Just before the Little Hillbillies record came out, we were playing at the Gympie Muster – in front of thousands of people. That's where Tal made his debut – he wandered on stage and said: 'This is a song I wrote because I have two houses. Sometimes I live at my mum's, sometimes I live at my dad's.' Everyone at that moment was thinking, 'Oh, poor boy.' He got to the point in the song where he sang the lyric, 'Lucky me,' and the crowd went crazy; it was so unexpected for them.

However, things don't always work out as planned. Tal also came on stage at the Deniliquin Ute Muster, another huge rural event. 'What song do you want to sing?' I asked him, hoping for a repeat of 'Two Houses'. 'I want to do "Eye of the Tiger",' he replied. Oh well.

I can see a lot of myself in the children. They're all so comfortable on stage; they can't wait to get out there, which was something I loved when I was their age – and still do. I don't look at them like some kind of stage mother. I don't analyse their singing or stagecraft anything like that. But I feel that they were born to have music around them, as Nash and I did as kids, and it fits them like a glove. Even at the age of two, you didn't have to persuade Arlo into going out on stage – he'd walk straight up to his microphone, sing, do his bit, then he'd tug on my skirt and ask me whether we can do 'Christmas Time'. He showed no sign of nerves at all. It's beautiful. I don't really mind what the kids choose to do with their lives; they don't have to become musicians. But right now they seem to be having a great time, which is more than enough for me.

Arlo, especially, is a real ham. He likes to stay around with me after shows. He'll sit on my hip while I'm signing autographs, and every time someone asks for a photo, no matter what kind of mood he's in, whether he's tired or cranky or hungry, as soon as that camera comes out he'll flash a big smile and shout: 'Cheese!' Every time. Wonder where he gets that from?

We recorded the Little Hillbillies album out at Nash's farm. You know that saying, 'Never work with kids and animals'? Now

I understand why. It was crazy. We recorded most of the music beforehand and then brought the kids in for a few days, bribing them when we needed them to sing. It was certainly the most fun I've had when making a record, but chaotic at the same time. Cori, who's an experienced film-maker, came out and filmed the chaos. The photo shoot for the album was crazier still; total bedlam, with these seven kids running everywhere and the photographer trying to get them in some kind of order. It came out surprisingly well.

We took the Little Hillbillies record out on the road, a little bit. We even incorporated it into a 'typical' gig – whatever that is – when we played at a Mudgee winery in October 2009. As I was playing I looked around me and realised I was absolutely swamped by my family. My dad was playing guitar to my right; Shane was to my left. Jeff McCormack, who's definitely part of my extended family, was playing bass, while John Watson, who drummed with us throughout the *Rattlin' Bones* period, was up back, keeping the beat. Mum and Ronnie were side-stage, doing their best to keep the kids – who were about to come on and sing – in some kind of order. Pete Dyball, our tech, who's been with us for a few years now, was working the foldback while Nash was doing 'front of house' sound.

Even Worm and Bern were there, in costume as 'Worm' and 'Froggles', characters from my children's book, although their roles were reversed. (It turned out that Bern, being taller than Worm, suited the worm outfit far better.) And then, on cue, all around me on stage was the next generation of the Chambers clan, including my boys Arlo and Tal. Despite our best efforts, there was no real organisation; the kids wandered on and off stage and grabbed a mic and sang when the mood hit. Chaos ruled at Little Hillbillies gigs, but in the best possible way. It was as though a typical day at my house was being played out on stage.

I'd said to Tal that we were going to be playing a gig at Mudgee, and asked if he wanted to come along. He'll grab any excuse to sing 'Two Houses', so he was totally up for it. But then he said: 'Mummy, it's Halloween – we won't be able to go out trick or treating.' We live in the kind of neighbourhood where people get into the spirit of Halloween. So I figured, well, let's bring Halloween to Mudgee and to the gig. So I had all the kids dress up in their costumes, rather than their usual Little Hillbillies outfits: Arlo was a skeleton, Tal was a zombie, Eden was the Grim Reaper, Skye was a witch. Very cute.

I'd bought a mountain of lollies beforehand, enough to keep a dentist in business for life, and took them around to the dressing rooms of the other acts on the bill – James Reyne, Mental as Anything, Wendy Matthews – and said, 'Look, my kids will be coming around trick or treating. Can you give them these?' So the kids trick-or-treated backstage, and they thought it was great.

The gig provided another one of my little 'moments' (I've had a few, as I think about it). I'd just played so much of my musical history, and then I was surrounded by my family and closest friends, playing the Hillbillies songs. It was as though my 'human jukebox' set closed the book on one part of my life and the Hillbillies set was documenting the next stage of my life. It felt really right.

I feel that every record really represents me at the time I make it. When we made *Rattlin' Bones*, Shane and I were recently married, and that was my whole life at that point. Now, my life is about being a mum, first and foremost, rather than being a musician, and the Little Hillbillies record gave me the chance to be both in the one project. I didn't care whether people thought it was lame or not cool. That's who I am, and I love it. I wanted to share our life at home with our kids with other people, but mostly I wanted to share music with my kids. It's great to know that music is there for them, in whatever way they may need it.

From time to time I would question whether I'd ever regain that songwriting spark that I had in my twenties, before the kids came along, but in March 2010 I had a huge creative burst. I wrote an entire album's worth of songs in a few weeks – they just came pouring out of me. It was fantastic and completely unexpected. Straight away I got on the phone to Nash and said, 'Let's book some studio time; I've got to record these songs.' Everyone felt good and right in their own way. They were a lot like the songs on *The Captain* and *Barricades*, yet seen through the eyes of me as I am now. I decided to produce the record with the help of my band, which was another first for me. Taking control, yet again.

I really had no plans for a new record. I was coasting and enjoying life as a wife and mother. But then – boom! – all of these songs hit me from, well, I don't know where. It was just as I was about to tour Australia with Texan troubadour Lyle Lovett.

Fortunately, I got the new songs out of my system and did the tour, which, incidentally, was one of the best I've ever been on. Lyle was a true gentleman, an intelligent, charming man, a great singer and musician – and he had an amazing band. And Lyle called me 'Ms Chambers', in that syrupy accent of his, which was kind of sweet.

But these new songs really were the biggest thing on my mind in early 2010, creatively speaking. We recorded in Nash's studio, where we did the Little Hillbillies record, and used a band I called the Millionaires. Shane and Dad played loads of stringed instruments, Jeff McCormack sat in on bass, John Watson drummed and Jim Moginie put his distinctive stamp on things.

Little Bird, the new album, was a link to my earlier records, and just like then, I wanted to invite along as many people as I could to help out. That's how I ended up with amazing cameos from people like Missy Higgins, who sang on 'Beautiful Mess', Camille Te Nahu, James Gillard, Kevin Bennett and Patty Griffin – the same Patty Griffin whose 'Top of the World' I'd sing while pregnant at the Lost Dogs. Patty helped out, fantastically well, with the song 'Somewhere', which is a bit of a sad one. But, hey, it's a country record, it's supposed to have sad songs.

The title track of *Little Bird* was the first song I wrote for this album and felt to me like the strong and secure version of 'Not Pretty Enough' a few years down the line – the whole album felt like that to me. I really wanted the record to reflect that old style I had; it was a lot like revisiting my songwriting past, except that the woman recording the songs was a bit older, and, hopefully, a

265

bit wiser. I wrote 'Not Pretty Enough' over ten years ago, at a time when I was being told that in order to be successful and fit in I'd have to change myself and my style. When I sat down to write the song 'Little Bird' I realised that I was glad that I didn't listen and that I stayed true to myself. In my opinion, there's way too much compromise in this industry.

There may have been a lot of echoes of my past, but I did take control in the studio – or at least I took as much control as I could. I heard all these songs in my head when I wrote them: the harmonies, the feel, the arrangements, so I really felt like it was time to try and produce my own record. I loved the challenge, even though Nash wouldn't let me touch the buttons in his studio. I don't blame him. So I was more like a traffic cop, directing the flow of the instruments and the recordings. Still, it was a great thrill to produce my own album.

I know that everyone says this when they make a record, but I genuinely think that *Little Bird* is the best thing I'd ever done. Or at least it's the most 'me' album that I've ever made; I truly feel like I get to know myself a little more with each album that I record. I had so much confidence while I was writing the songs for *Little Bird*, and they just fell out so naturally, as it should be, and that carried through into the studio. I love the songs and have loved playing them live. The whole experience has given me this new energy as a songwriter and as a musician. I feel stronger and more powerful now than I did back in my early solo career. Hopefully that came through in the song 'Little Bird' and the entire album.

I really enjoy the luxury of being able to do something creatively when an idea hits me, rather than being tied to a schedule. The Little Hillbillies record was a classic example of me being totally inspired by an idea – okay, Dad's idea – and then jumping into the project headfirst. Likewise *Little Bird*. If I have any kind of criteria nowadays, that would be it; whatever I do I'll do because I'm inspired and it excites me, not because I feel that have to do it.

As I sit and write this and reflect on my life so far, I realise that I have no regrets. Even the stuff that I should regret, I don't. I now understand that all my mistakes, as well as my successes, ultimately add up to make the person that I am today. I'm comfortable in my own skin, which hasn't always been the case. And I feel like I still have tons of new songs in me, loads of music that'll come out in time. But priorities change – and you slowly grow up. And I'd be the first person to admit that I've still got a lot of growing up to do. No matter where my life leads me, I can't wait for whatever comes next.

Credits

KASEY CHAMBERS has won eight Australian Record Industry Association awards, 10 Australian Performing Right Association awards, 18 Country Music Association of Australia awards and has sold more than 1.5 million albums. She lives on the NSW Central Coast with her husband and two children, with a third due in October 2011.

www.kaseychambers.com

JEFF APTER is the author of 11 books. His latest is the bestselling *Together Alone: The Story of the Finn Brothers*.

www.jeffapter.com.au

Nullarbor, The Biggest Backyard

When I was a little girl
I had the biggest backyard in the world
It went on for miles and miles, was wide as it was high
Down to the horizon, all the way up to the sky
And every now and then
I heard a myall tree cry my name

When I was a little girl
I had the biggest backyard in the world

Covered up with red dirt as far as I could see
I shared it with the railway and the Aborigines
Southwest of Ooldea
All the way down to the sea and back

When I was a little girl
I had the biggest backyard in the world

The sun would shine until the day I asked for it to rain
Counting down the sleeps until the Tea and Sugar train
Ten cents on the track for days
Before it ever came and went

When I was a little girl
I had the biggest backyard in the world

Sitting 'round the campfire that started from a spark
Rolling down the Gun Barrel Highway in the dark
Making sure that I had all the room here in my house
For me and all of the world

When I was a little girl
I had the biggest backyard in the world

KASEY CHAMBERS Album discography

With The Dead Ringer Band

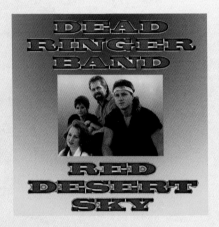

Red Desert Sky

(Larrikin 1993)

___

Road to Nowhere/Born in the
Country/Power of the Land/Ashes
of Love/Wish You Were Here
/Too Many Blues in This Room
/Wild Turkey/Red Desert
Sky/Baby Don't Go/Northern
Highway/Sweetest Gift/Last Days
on the Road/Won't Be Needing
You/Itchy Twitchy Spot

Home Fires

(Massive 1995)

___

Home Fires/More About Love
/Always Be Me/Australian Son
/Honky Tonk From Hell/I'd Go
Home If I Had One/Why?/Family
Man/Burning Flame/Just Wanted
to See You So Bad/Sin City/Guitar
Talk/Gypsy Bound

Living in the Circle

(Massive 1997)

Too Confused/Living in the
Circle/Halfway to Sydney/Things
Don't Come Easy/That's What
Makes a Broken Heart/The Last
Generation/If I Needed You
/Too Many Friends/Life's Little
Mysteries/Already Gone/Loop
Around Atlanta/No Depression
/Am I the Only One/Just like
Yesterday (song for Gram)

Hopeville

(Massive 1998)

Born to Run/Sometimes She
Forgets/TB Blues/Hello Hopeville
/Speed of the Sound of
Loneliness/Return of the Grievous
Angel/I Wish It Would Rain/Crazy
Heart/White Freight Liner Blues
/He Thinks I Still Care/Leaving
Louisiana in the Broad Daylight
/Something About What Happens
When We Talk

Solo

The Captain

(EMI 1999)

_____

Cry Like a Baby/The Captain/This
Flower/You Got the Car/These
Pines/Don't Talk Back/Southern
Kind of Life/Mr Baylis/Hard Way
/Last Hard Bible/Don't Go/We're
All Gonna Die Someday

**Highest Australian Chart
Position: #11; 3 x platinum**

Barricades & Brickwalls

(EMI 2001)

_____

Barricades & Brickwalls
/Not Pretty Enough/On a Bad
Day/Runaway Train/Little Bit
Lonesome/Nullarbor Song/Million
Tears/Still Feeling Blue/This
Mountain/Crossfire/Falling Into
You/If I Were/I Still Pray

**Highest Australian Chart
Position: #1; 7 x platinum**

Wayward Angel

(EMI 2003)

Pony/Hollywood/Stronger
/Bluebird/More Than Ordinary
/Wayward Angel/Paper
Aeroplane/Cry Like a River/For
Sale/Follow You Home/Mother
/Guilty As Sin/Lost and Found
/Saturated

**Highest Australian Chart
Position: #1; 3 x platinum**

Carnival

(EMI 2006)

Colour of a Carnival/Sign on
the Door/Rain/Light up a
Candle/Hard Road/Nothing at
All/Railroad/I Got You Now/
Dangerous/Surrender/You Make
Me Sing/Don't Look So Sad

**Highest Australian Chart
Position: #1; platinum**

Rattlin' Bones

with Shane Nicholson

(Liberation 2008)

Rattlin' Bones/Once in a While
/Sweetest Waste of Time/Monkey
on a Wire/One More Year
/The House That Never Was
/Wildflower/No One Hurts up
Here/The Devil's Inside My Head
/Sleeping Cold/Adeline/Jackson
Hole/Your Day Will Come/Woe
Is Mine

**Highest Australian Chart
Position: #1; platinum**

Kasey Chambers, Poppa Bill and the Little Hillbillies

(Liberation 2009)

The Lost Music Blues/The Ballad
of Poppa Bill/I Spy/Poppa Bill
Says/Dad, Do You Remember?
/Before You Came Along/Two
Houses/Old Man Down on the
Farm/My Oh My/When We Were
Kids/Sometimes/Something in
the Water/Imagination/Blue
/Christmas Time/The Best Years

Little Bird

(Liberation 2010)

Someone Like Me/Beautiful Mess
/Devil on Your Back/Little Bird
/Georgia Brown/Somewhere
/This Story/Love Like a Hurricane
/Down Here on Earth/Nullarbor,
the Biggest Backyard/Bring Back
My Heart/Invisible Girl/Train
Wreck/The Stupid Things I Do

**Highest Australian Chart
Position: #3; gold**

Little Bird

A little bird told me late last night that if I hold my breath and do everything right
You might come back
If I colour my hair and I wear it down and I make you laugh like a circus clown
You might come back
And a little bird said with the wink of an eye if I beg real hard and I do not cry
You might come back
If I keep my opinion under my breath and I only bring it out when the master says
You might come back

But I don't want you that bad
No I don't want you that bad

But a little bird told me as plain as day if I changed my name and I change my way
You might come back
If I sell my soul for the greater cause
If I burn my records and I listen to yours
You might come back
And a little bird said in the middle of a dream if I shut my mouth and I don't make a scene
You might come back
If I crossed my fingers and curl my toes
If I looked liked the other girls
Everybody knows
You might come back

But I don't want you that bad
No I don't want you that bad
No I don't want you that bad
No I don't want you that bad

A little bird told me
A little bird told me